INGE SKOVGAARD

The
Technique of
Tønder Lace

INGE SKOVGAARD

The
Technique of
Tønder Lace

B.T. Batsford Ltd · London

First published 1991

ISBN 0 7134 6255 8

Typeset by Servis Filmsetting Limited,
Manchester
And printed by
Butler & Tanner Ltd Frome, Somerset
For the Publisher
B. T. Batsford Limited
4 Fitzhardinge Street
London W1H 0AH

A catalogue record for this book is available
from the British Library

1 (previous page) Four lacemakers outside a
house in Rørkær, c. 1885 (Institut for Sønderjysk
Lokalhistorie, Aabenraa)

Contents

Acknowledgements

Without help from various quarters it would have been impossible to write this book. Therefore I should like to thank the staff at Tønder Museum for their helpfulness when I needed to study old patterns in order to make reconstructions. I also want to express my thanks to the staff at the Museum at Koldinghus and to Charlotte Paludan at the Museum of Decorative Art in Copenhagen for their readiness to help me. And finally my thanks go to those lacemakers who earlier made up the reconstructions to the patterns 2, 3, 4, 7, 10, 17, 18, 19 and 48, all of which I got from my teacher of Tønder lace, Sina Kielberg, many years ago.

I am most grateful to the family from Lorenzen's Gaard, Ballum for permission to use their reconstruction as a guide, when I worked out the diagram and pricking to 'Stinne Winther'. The use of samplers as an introduction to Tønder lace is an idea from a course in Ballum. Anna Kjems was very helpful to me with information and encouragement.

For the illustrations listed below I am grateful to the following: 1, photograph by kind permission of the Institut for Sønderjysk Lokalhistorie; 2, photograph by kind permission of the Royal Danish Collections at Rosenborg, photographer Lennart Larsen; 3, map of the lace district, drawn by my daughter Ingrid Skovgaard; 4, 5, 6, 8 and 13, photographs by kind permission of Nationalmuseet's Billedarkiv, Dansk Folkemuseum (Nat. Mus.), photographer Niels Elswing; and 9, photograph by kind permission of Langelands Museum. I want to thank the photographers Hans and Pylle Aps, Copenhagen, for their enthusiastic work with the photographs on the jacket.

I should like to express my gratitude to Pamela Nottingham, whose books have been very useful when lace terms needed to be clarified.

Similar gratitude must go to my two first lace teachers, Esther and Edith Andreassen, who taught me lacemaking without diagrams, but with just a photocopy or a sample as a guide. This working method has facilitated the making of the reconstructions.

Friends and family have been very helpful to me by pointing out the worst blunders in the text and giving me the necessary criticism. I am most grateful to all of them, especially to my husband, Tham Skovgaard, whose patience has been severely taxed.

Foreword

When you are going to write a book it is necessary to do a good deal of research to get the book as satisfactory and interesting as possible. So, in connection with this book, I had to procure all relevant books and articles that might help me to get a vivid picture of the heyday of the Tønder lace industry. Simultaneously I looked through my prickings and old pieces of lace, and I visited museums with collections of lace in order to find a representative selection of patterns.

One might have chosen to gather patterns from all periods of Tønder lace making, but as Tønder lace is associated mostly with the period from 1800 to 1850 I have concentrated on the lace from these years. The patterns are mostly of the Lille type, adapted to the new, Danish surroundings and way of life. A few others are included too, because they were made in great quantities from *c.*1850 to *c.*1900.

I found it impossible to put the patterns consistently in order of difficulty from the easiest to the most complicated. The first patterns are the easiest ones, but for the rest I have tried to put them in groups of related designs and techniques, bringing in each group an explanation of the new technique.

It has been a fascinating experience to become so absorbed in the lace that I saw lace patterns in carpets and wallpapers and dreamt about them at night. In a way it has been a little frightening too, because I found so many unknown details that eventually I had to admit, like Socrates, 'I know nothing'. But I have learnt from the work, and my hope is that I have learnt enough to give other lacemakers some knowledge of Tønder lace, an understanding of my love of the old patterns, and the opportunity to work some of the examples I have chosen, not always because of their beauty, but also to show the versatility of Tønder lace as it developed over a short space of time.

—1—

The history of Tønder lace

The sixteenth and seventeenth centuries

When we talk about the lace industry in a certain area, we always ask: When did it start? Where did the idea come from? Why did it become an industry here of all places? In Denmark we ask these questions about the Tønder lace industry, but it is not always possible to get a satisfactory answer. A bobbin found buried in the ground, and a letter of 1595, in which a lady asks her daughter in Tønder to send her the lace she had ordered, are some of the first proofs of lacemaking around Tønder, so no doubt the beginning was in the sixteenth century.

Some events seem to show that some sort of relationship between merchants and lacemakers was established around the beginning of the seventeenth century. Firstly, it is written in the Records of the Courts of Tønder, 1622, that a lacemaker who did not fulfil her obligations towards the lace merchant had been employed by him since 1613. Secondly, King Christian IV wrote in his diary in 1619, that he met several lace merchants in Valsbøl, a village a little west of Flensborg, and bought lace and linen for 889 rigsdalers (old Danish coin).

This information demands an explanation of the special political conditions in the south of Jutland. For about five centuries the province between two small rivers, the Kongeaa and the Ejder, was used by alternating sovereigns as a sort of commodity. Sometimes it was given as security, if the king wanted money; sometimes it was given as a duchy to one of the king's relatives. It was united and then divided into several shares of inheritance, and finally it was dismembered in small parts, some owned by the king, some by the dukes, and some ruled in common. Valsbøl, where, in fact, no lace merchants lived, was situated in one of the common parts, so it was possible for the king to meet people there without treading on anybody's toes.

We cannot establish that the lace on the clothes of Christian IV is Danish, but tradition tells that it is. The lace made in the province of Slesvig was of exactly the same style as in the rest of Europe, beginning with plaited lace in the sixteenth century and developing into patterns with large, beautiful scallops in the seventeenth century.

About 1386, when parts of the province were given as a fief to Gert, Count of Holsten, 'Slesvig' became the name of the province. When the lace industry arose, the lace was not called Tønder lace but 'lace of Slesvig'.

People in the west of Slesvig have always had to fight against the North Sea. They built dikes to protect the land against the waves

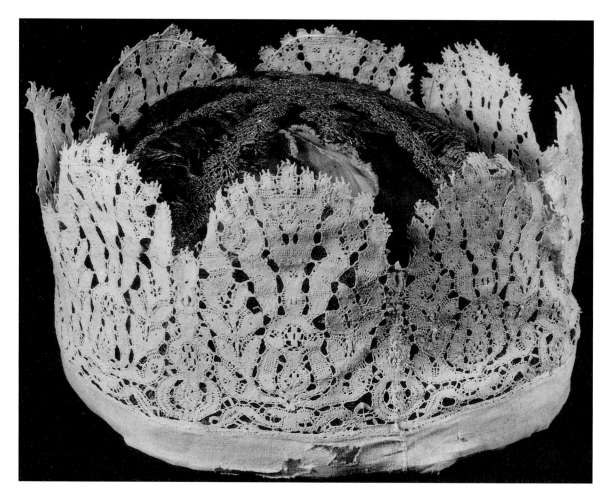

2 King Christian IV's night cap (The Royal Danish Collections at Rosenborg. Photographer: Lennart Larsen)

and more dikes in an attempt to gain new land. During the last half of the sixteenth and the beginning of the seventeenth centuries they succeeded so well that Tønder, a commercial centre of Slesvig, was some distance from the sea. Losing this means of communication the merchants of Tønder had to find new modes of operation; and as they saw that lace was going to be the fashion of the future, they ventured to put their money into the trade. The roads going south were good, commercial and cultural connections

had been established long before, and as the farming of the area did not require women's help as much as usual at that time, it was easy to get the necessary workforce.

The lacemaking district proper was very small, indicated on the map with a solid line, but when the industry boomed, during the eighteenth and the beginning of the nineteenth centuries, the district stretched a good deal farther, indicated with a dot-and-dash line. You may wonder why such a

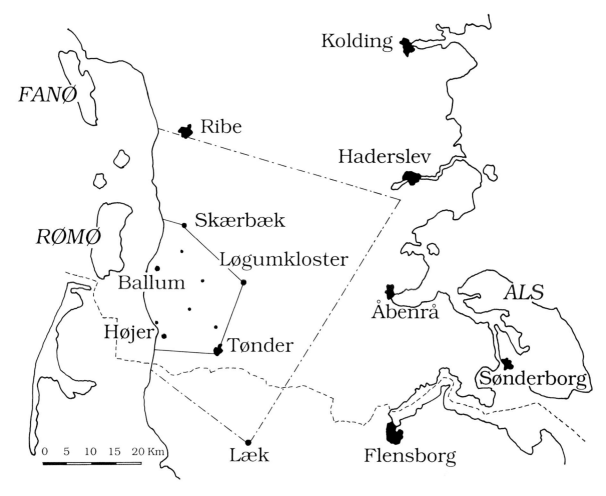

3   Map of the lace district (Ingrid Skovgaard)

prosperous industry did not spread further, but as mentioned above, the conditions in western Slesvig were ideal, there was a sort of border between Slesvig and the rest of the country where travellers had to pay duty, and—possibly the most important reason—the merchants of Tønder held on to the industry and kept the lacemakers bound to the locality.

It is not known exactly when the industry became properly organized. A merchant named Johan Steinbeck came from the south, possibly from Westphalia, to Tønder about 1647. He has been considered the father of

the lace industry of Slesvig, but that is not in fact true. There were lace merchants before Steinbeck, but no doubt he was a very skilled merchant and an essential contributor to the organization and growth of the trade. The most certain proof of an industry of a considerable size is given in a map dated 1648 of the Tønder area, in which the cartographer Johannes Mejer from Husum has placed in the cartouche a lady with a piece of lace in her hands, showing it to the onlooker.

Our knowledge of the lace industry in the rest of the century is very slight, and not

much lace is left to tell us more. Towards the end of the century some lighter patterns were produced, often with pointed scallops.

The eighteenth century

As early as 1683 King Christian V issued a decree, that the nobility and persons of rank were allowed to wear only 'white and black lace, made in this country'. An endless line of prohibitions and orders followed during the eighteenth century with the main purpose of protecting the trade. In 1736 it was once more forbidden to wear foreign lace. Offenders were fined 200 rigsdalers, half of which was given to the informer. In 1769 the prohibition was repeated, but this time the fine was the same amount as the value of the lace. The lace, of course, was confiscated. These prohibitions were cancelled in 1797, and in their place heavy duties were introduced on all foreign lace—only the lace of Slesvig was free of duty.

How it was possible to tell the difference between home-produced and foreign lace is not easy to understand, particularly as the lace of Slesvig was sometimes sold abroad as 'Brabant goods'. This was not surprising as the lace industry had to follow the fashion in Europe, so the patterns were imitations of Flemish lace, or were bought in Brabant, together with the very fine linen thread essential for a satisfactory result. In the beginning Binche lace was the model, with patterns as beautiful as ice-ferns on window panes. Later on, towards the end of the century, the gimp was introduced under the

4   Late seventeenth-century lace (Nationalmuseet's Billedarkiv, Dansk Folkemuseum. Photographer: Niels Elswing)

5   (right) Early eighteenth-century lace (Nationalmuseet's Billedarkiv, Dansk Folkemuseum. Photographer: Niels Elswing)

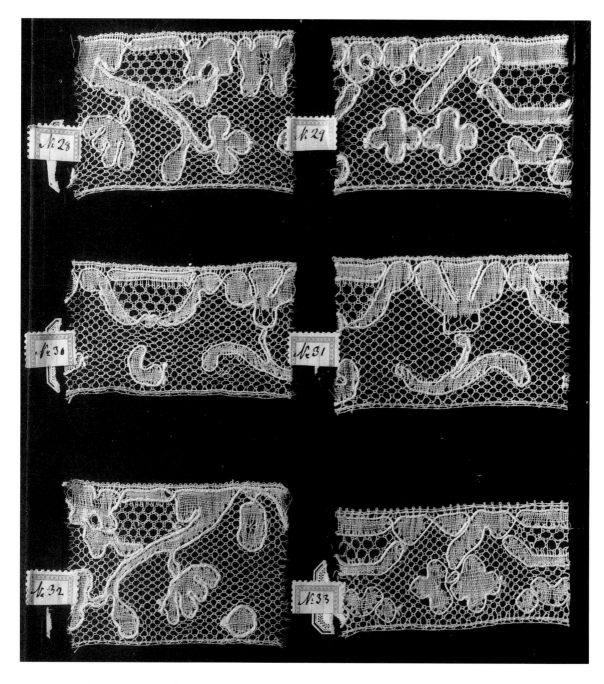

6 *Late eighteenth-century lace*
(Nationalmuseet's Billedarkiv, Dansk
Folkemuseum. Photographer: Niels Elswing)

a

b

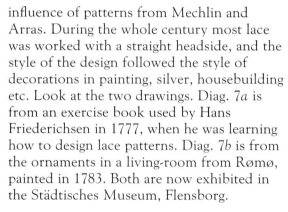

*7a&b Late eighteenth-century patterns, for lace (**a**) and painting (**b**)*

influence of patterns from Mechlin and Arras. During the whole century most lace was worked with a straight headside, and the style of the design followed the style of decorations in painting, silver, housebuilding etc. Look at the two drawings. Diag. 7a is from an exercise book used by Hans Friederichsen in 1777, when he was learning how to design lace patterns. Diag. 7b is from the ornaments in a living-room from Rømø, painted in 1783. Both are now exhibited in the Städtisches Museum, Flensborg.

There were continual conflicts between the lace merchants—or lace manufacturers as they were mostly called—and the pedlars, and between these two parties and the Department of Commerce of the Danish government. The trade was growing fast during the eighteenth century and at one time about 12,000 lacemakers were employed—the figure 16,000 has been mentioned. With so many lacemakers throughout the area working in their homes, the manufacturers had to be skilled in the artistic as well as the commercial side of their trade. On behalf of his colleagues, a well-known manufacturer, Hans Richtsen, wrote a long statement of what ought to be required of a lace manufacturer in 1761. This is a summary.

- He must have learnt the art of drawing to make patterns himself, and he must have established good relations with people in Brabant in order to get new ideas from there.
- He must be able to choose the most saleable patterns.
- He must be able to teach the lacemakers, when he has got something new.
- He has to know how to distribute the patterns to the lacemakers, according to their god-given abilities.
- He must be able to point out any mistakes in the work and know how to help the lacemaker.
- He must be able to find the right thread for every pattern, and in the same way to find the particular thread that suits each lacemaker best.
- He must make sure that he is well supplied with beautiful patterns.
- And he must possess some commercial experience and have established commercial contacts abroad.

To achieve these skills, he states, an apprenticeship of seven years is desirable. Hans Richtsen ends up his statement with a complaint against the pedlars. They might be useful, he says, because the merchant is not always able to travel with the lace himself.

He must stay at home to attend to the lacemakers and supply them with thread and patterns and give them their pay, when they come to have their lace cut off. But he wants the prefect of the county to stop the pedlars, who in his opinion do not know enough about lacemaking and trade, doing the rounds of the lacemakers and offering them a little more for their lace than they are likely to get from the manufacturer. It is easy to understand the anger and annoyance among the manufacturers, but their pleas were not heeded by the authorities. The latter realized that it served the interests of the lacemakers best if the manufacturers faced some competition; otherwise the lacemakers would have earned even less than they did.

It must have been a hard job to be a pedlar. They walked for miles with their knapsacks on their backs in all weathers. But no doubt they were welcome wherever they came. After some years on the roads, when they had made a fortune for themselves, it often happened that they settled as manufacturers, without having served their apprenticeship, but with simply peddling experience to fall back on. Now it was their turn to complain about the pedlars, when they encroached on their territory.

While manufacturers travelled long distances to buy thread and patterns, to sell lace, and to find new marketing possibilities, the lacemakers were rooted to the spot as mentioned above. Firstly, they were connected with one manufacturer, from whom they got their materials and to whom, mostly, they delivered their lace. Secondly, they were not allowed to leave the province according to an edict of 1740. All ports and roads were watched to prevent the lacemakers from 'deserting' and perhaps founding a new lace industry in another place. Not only lacemakers, but all travellers had to have a passport, but the edict was introduced in the first place to control lacemakers' movements. As one can imagine, the rules could not always be kept. Sometimes mercenaries were quartered in Tønder—inevitably soldiers and lacemakers sometimes fell in love and were married, and you could not forbid a wife to follow her husband when he went home. Of course the Tønder local authorities complained about the quartering!

In spite of these quarrels the industry expanded during the eighteenth century. It is impossible to know the exact number of lace merchants, because many of them sold goods other than lace and were registered as merchants without lace being mentioned. But the trade was large, in some years larger even than the cattle trade. The lace of Slesvig was sold in Denmark-Norway, in Germany and other European countries, and even as far away as Russia. The growing trade resulted in the establishment of two linen thread factories in 1769 and 1792 with the purpose of keeping the money in the province. Both factories existed until 1834, when the competition from cotton thread became too fierce.

Cotton was considered new in the nineteenth century, but the fact is that even in 1606 cotton was being spun in an orphanage in Copenhagen. It was founded by Christian IV and was accorded royal privilege. For 30 years many orphan girls and daughters of very poor parents learnt spinning and lacemaking in the orphanage. It is not known if the lace was made of cotton, but the accounts demonstrate that it was very much appreciated by the court. In 1611 40 alens were delivered for 'the collars of his Royal Majesty' (one alen is about two feet [60 centimetres]). The girls were 'released' in 1641 and nothing is known about their lot subsequently. The whole establishment was closed shortly after the King's death in 1648. Cotton thread was forgotten and not reinvented until the nineteenth century.

The first half of the nineteenth century

When cotton thread was introduced in Slesvig, the lace industry was already declining. The number of lace merchants in Tønder was 13 by about 1800, and in 1836 only one was left. More lace merchants lived in the country, but only six are known of in 1847. In 1812 about 12,000 lacemakers were still working in the Tønder area, but by 1847 only about 1,500 were registered as lacemakers associated with a lace merchant. The lace was mostly sold in Denmark—only a few maintained their relations with other countries.

The best-known merchant from these years is Jens Wulff in Brede, about 10 miles (15 kilometres) north of Tønder. He sold his lace and other goods, wool, cattle, corn etc. in Denmark and abroad, and even to the United States, which, in 1832, he saw as the best market for the lace trade. For many years he wrote a diary and every New Year's Eve he made a summary of the year, and we can follow the lot of the lace industry with the aid of his figures and comments.

As the use of lace is subject to the whims of fashion, it is no wonder that lace industries all over Europe were on the decline in these years. The French Revolution left its mark on dress at the same time as machine-made lace gained ground, both being injurious to the lace industry. But different circumstances extended the life of the Tønder lace industry. The thread from local factories was cheaper than the Flemish thread; it was also coarser, and so the patterns could not be made in so refined and so elaborate a form as before: this enabled the lacemakers to work faster. Furthermore, a new market was opened: Danish peasant women began to use lace on their bonnets.

Lille lace, fashionable at that time, became the model with the point ground as the background to the figures and a gimp to emphasize the design. The structure of the industry had changed and lacemakers were freer to work in their own way. The lace of Slesvig had an 'Indian Summer' with domestic garden flowers flourishing on the lace pillows. This lace, which old lacemakers called 'half stitch lace', is the one we consider 'real' Tønder lace.

8   A crosscloth from Agersø, south of Korsør (Nationalmuseet's Billedarkiv, Dansk Folkemuseum. Photographer: Niels Elswing)

Shortly before the middle of the century it was obvious to Jens Wulff that lace schools were needed to support the industry, and he established two himself. The need for more

9 *One way to wear a crosscloth (Langelands Museum. Drawing by Frederik Kruse, 1850)*

schools was examined and generally accepted. But Holsten and parts of Slesvig rebelled against the Kingdom of Denmark and in 1848 a war broke out between Denmark and Germany which lasted for three years. The lace schools were forgotten.

We do not know much about the lacemakers of the seventeenth and eighteenth centuries.

Most of our knowledge comes from the Court Records and from a letter written by one old woman who felt that she had been exploited by the lace merchant. Certainly lacemakers were not wealthy, but neither were other ordinary people. In the nineteenth century the lacemakers' lives are more clearly recorded, but views of their lives differed: some people thought that the lacemakers led a rather pleasant life, others that their conditions were miserable.

In 1815 Knud Aagaard, a vicar of Agerskov, about 20 miles (30 kilometres) north east of Tønder, described his surroundings, including the life of a lacemaker. He wrote about the women who learnt to make lace but nothing else. The husbands worked at the spinning-wheel and in the kitchen; some of them knitted stockings for the family, because the lacemakers did not know how to knit. During the summer, girls from Jutland were hired to work in the fields, so that the housewives could stay at the pillow. I must add that it was not always like that. Most women were only part-time lacemakers and saw to their households themselves, but the full-time lacemakers were the most skilled and got the best pay for their work. Knud Aagaard tells that they spent their money on luxuries such as coffee, sugar, snuff, and fine clothes, and who can blame them!

Steen Steensen Blicher, a vicar and poet in northern Jutland mostly known for his short stories, wrote that the lacemaker is 'the silkworm of the lace merchant; he wants the silk and cares little about the butterfly'. A very pessimistic view, but with some truth.

The lacemakers took up their profession early in life and had to learn it for six years. Why not let a lacemaker herself tell about her life? In 1889 another vicar, Henning

10 *Early nineteenth-century lace (enlarged)*

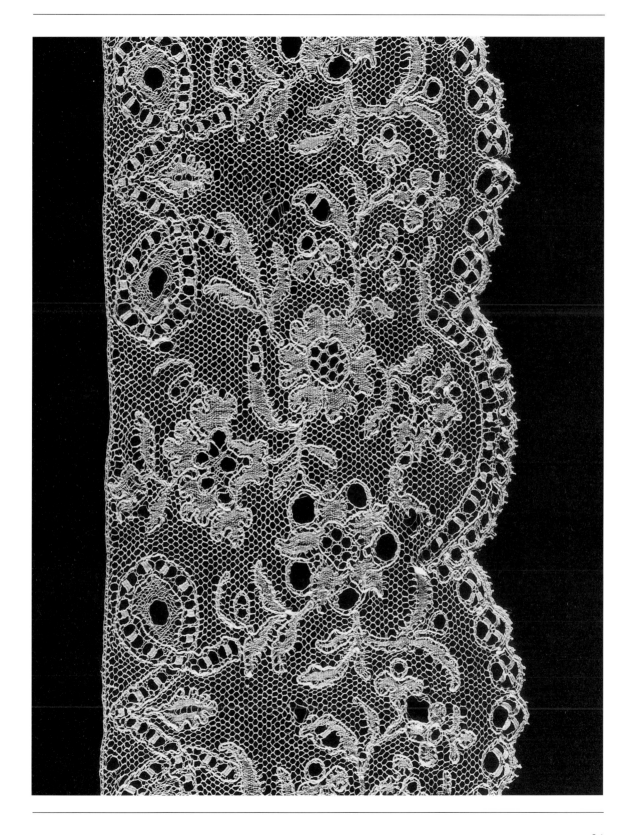

Frederick Feilberg, who lived in Darum, a little north of Ribe, published a book on *Danish Peasant Life*, and he asks an old lacemaker, Ane Marie, if she can tell him how she learned to make lace. She answers:

Yes, of course I can. Nearly all of us around Møgeltønder made lace, but we had to begin very early to learn the 'stitch', and I was barely eight years old when I started. I came to an old couple, quiet people, and the wife made lace; later on we even had a school, where more than a score of children were together. You ask if the schoolmaster liked it—well, my mother was very scrupulous and I didn't miss one day of school. In the junior class we went to school three days a week all the year round and the other three days to lace school; when I advanced to the senior class I had to go only two days a week, and then I was four days in lace school.

We started with the narrow patterns and a few bobbins and we didn't have a big 'lace case' but a 'stork's nest'; it was a flat rectangular piece of wood with four holes, one in each corner; four sticks were stuck into those holes and on top of them was the pillow with the pricking, the pattern on which we made lace. The whole arrangement rested on our knees and we leant the outer edge of the case against a stand. It was on a sort of stool and we could take it up and down as we needed. In the evening we used a lamp. At that time we used small lamps with some sort of oil and as they didn't give a particularly good light, each of us four girls, sitting round one lamp, had a glass ball with water hanging in front of her such as the shoemakers use; this ball too could be moved up or down, so we were always able to make the light shine on our work. And though I was still a child I earned more than one batch of bread for my family.

When we were grown up we used to meet and work four together; we could save both lighting and heating in this way, you know. Then it might happen that some young men came in; and we young people certainly enjoyed ourselves in those days. Then we might say: 'Come again another evening and we will invite you for our "stand-feast".' The young men came at least two evenings a week; they usually came at dusk when they had got their supper and they stayed until about nine o'clock when they had to go home and take care of the cattle. They told us news from the village or old fairy-tales; and some of them could sing and we had many beautiful ballads at that time.

When the evening gatherings stopped we girls made a little feast, a 'stand-feast', and invited the young men who had kept us company; it was a very simple feast, they got a cup of coffee with rusks and some sandwiches and thanks in addition, because they had whiled away time for us during the long winter evenings.

I earned a good deal of money with my bobbins—at times they gave a very good income. With a piece of lace finished we might go to the great lace merchant Hansen in Møgeltønder; he supplied us with thread and afterwards he paid us according to the length of the lace. We always got silver coins, because they had no bank notes there at that time, and we came in one by one and got our money. He didn't like to have more than one girl at a time in his room; there might be those to whom he paid more for the same pattern, because the work was so beautiful; others were careless and got less. He didn't want us to chat about that; but I really think he must have had silver coins galore, when I

11 *Late nineteenth-century lappet*

consider how many people might come in one day. We were allowed to come whenever we wanted to, but before Christmas, Easter, and Whitsun all of us came. Even in the old days the prices went up and down, but I don't think the laces have ever given such a small profit as they do today.

The evening gatherings started in September and stopped towards the middle of March.

After 1850

Hansen, the 'great lace merchant' mentioned by Ane Marie, must be Dines Hansen, one of six merchants who were still working in the lace trade in 1847. Jens Wulff died in 1858 and his two sons continued in the business, but after the war between Denmark and Germany in 1864 they gave up, and only one 'old-fashioned' lace merchant, Ditlev Hansen, carried on until his death in 1909. About 1850 the style of the lace changed once more, now influenced by Swedish lace and by older and coarser types of lace. After 1864, when Denmark was forced to surrender Slesvig to Germany, the influence came from Germany too. It was not possible for the lacemakers to earn their living exclusively by lacemaking and many of them did not want their work to be sold in Berlin as German lace, so they put away their pillows, bobbins and patterns. They were also anxious to prevent them being bought by German museums and societies. Throughout the centuries lacemaking was always considered a *Danish* industry (both in Denmark and internationally).

However, some lacemakers needed the little money they could earn and they went on, even though they had to sell their work to the Germans, and sometimes they only got the same pay for a yard (metre) as they earlier had got for an alen (two feet [60 centimetres]). The metric system was introduced in Germany about 1870. The lacemakers worked Torchon lace and I have been told that they did not even have time to look up from the pillow to welcome a visitor; the day's work had to be finished.

There was a saying among the old lacemakers: The Tønder lace is asleep; it cannot die—it will wake up again to a new life. In 1908 an exhibition was held in the Danish Museum of Decorative Art with about 1,400 pieces of lace on display. The museum keeper, Emil Hannover, wrote a book linked with the exhibition and referred to lacemaking as 'the dying industry'. This made Hansigne Lorenzen, an author and farmer's wife in Ballum, set about saving lacemaking. She went to the old lacemakers and asked them to find their old patterns and try to remember how to use them. The fact that she was a member of the Danish minority in Germany complicated her work and not until 1920, when the northern part of Slesvig became Danish again, could she travel freely. But step by step, working as a lace merchant, she succeeded in 'reviving' the lace; almost as if a pattern had to be called by its own name to become alive, the lacemakers began to use names. In the old days the patterns were numbered in the sample books of the merchants, and the lacemakers might refer to a pattern as 'the 24-bobbin lace'. But from about 1900 many patterns were given names, such as the name of a lacemaker, a place name, or the name of a flower.

Nowadays the work is carried on by lacemakers who are deeply fascinated by the unique beauty of the 'lace of Slesvig'.

—2—

Equipment

Old tools are fascinating. They say much about the craft, about industry, and about the pleasure to be found in producing something beautiful.

The Tønder lace case

The lacemakers in Slesvig did not use the usual roller pillow, but a 'lace case' without a roller. This consists of a wooden plate, 20–24in. (50–60cm) long and 15–20in. (40–50cm) broad, with a curved incision in the end facing the lacemaker. The plate is covered with leather or fabric—oilcloth may be seen too—and stuffed with hay, preferably from fields so far from the sea that there is no salt in the hay. The plate with the pillow on the top is fixed on a case with a slanting surface with the low end facing the lacemaker. In the other end, about 8in. (20cm) high, there may be a little compartment with a shutter, and in the sides one or two drawers, used for spare bobbins, thread, and other necessities.

The surface of the lace case was held in a nearly horizontal position. The curved incision rested in the lap and the other end on a stand. The length of the stand could be changed as required by the lacemaker, and as the stand was on a little stool she could rest her feet on the stool and sit comfortably at the work. Some lacemakers preferred to

work without a stand (photo. 1).

The lace case has some accessories. Two 'side pieces' of leather with big holes were placed along the sides of the pillow from the top and about halfway down. The holes took the divider pins which kept the bobbins not being used for the moment in order and away from the work. Sometimes old and worn prickings were used as side pieces, if nothing else was available. Across the pillow is quite a big piece of leather, the 'working piece', on which the bobbins in use are resting. It is also called a 'skræwel', because 'skræwel' in the local dialect means 'chat'— the bobbins are 'chatting' while they work! The working piece can be moved up and down by means of straps and small pegs put into holes in the underside of the wooden plate. In the middle, between the side pieces, the pricking is fixed, sewn onto a padded piece of fabric a little bigger than the pricking. Between the pricking and the side pieces there may be two 'middle pieces' of oil-cloth. A corset bone or thin bamboo stick is placed across the pricking to lift up the threads away from the rough parchment and protect them from being worn. There is also a pin cushion, stuffed with wool, and a string of beads with a pair of scissors hanging at the end. Everything has to be within arm's reach.

The lace cases were not professionally made. Local carpenters or relatives made them; that

12 *Tønder lace case dating from 1786, restored for exhibition 1931 (Nationalmuseet's Billedarkiv, Dansk Folkemuseum. Photographer: Niels Elswing)*

is probably why they are so variable in their proportions. Some are plain, but usually they are painted in a beautiful colour, maybe with flowers, with the initials of the lacemaker, or with the year of the making. Sometimes the decoration is carved.

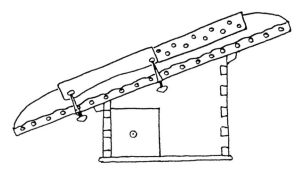

13 Tønder lace case, seen from the side

The lacemakers used different cloths with the case. They used a little one to wrap around the finished lace to keep it clean, another one to cover the lace if they left the work for a short time, and a bigger one to cover the bobbins and keep them in their places, if a longer break in the work was necessary. A very important cloth was the 'setting-up cloth'. Every time the pricking was filled—when the lacemaker had 'done her down'—she had to take out the pins, move the lace to the top of the pricking, and put in a sufficient number of pins again. To be able to do this she used the setting-up cloth. It was put in under the bobbins, folded around them like a bag and fixed with strong pins before the lace was loosened from the pricking. The cloth was not taken away again until enough pins were put in for the lace to stand the pull of the bobbins. To me, used to a roller pillow, this seems rather laborious, but I have been told by a lacemaker who always works on an old-fashioned lace case that it gives no problems. When the lacemaker left her work overnight or for a longer period, she used the 'big cloth' to cover the whole arrangement; many of these were beautiful scarves.

Bobbins

The old bobbins from Slesvig meet all demands you may make on a bobbin to be used with fine thread. They are nice and easy to handle and they look beautiful. No wonder they were used as gifts for a sweetheart. Locally they were called 'sticks'. A typical Tønder bobbin has a short spool with very small discs in the ends. There is enough room for the thin thread, and the small discs are a help when you need to use many bobbins in a pattern because they do not catch on neighbouring threads. The shank is thin, cylindrical, and often with incisions in different patterns. The handle in the end is usually shaped as a ball, but it may be flattened or stretched and decorated with incisions, paint and beads. The beads are not only for decoration. They add a little weight to the bobbins and prevent the wood from being worn by rubbing against the leather.

The oldest bobbins were simple, mostly turned of local wood. Today their ball-shaped handles are so worn that they appear cylindrical, like bobbin *a* in diag. 14. Later on the makers gave them incisions, coloured with red and green paint. Nowadays these bobbins are hard to find, probably because they are very elaborate and were never made in great quantities. Unfortunately, the pattern is worn away very quickly (bobbin *b*). Glass is much harder than wood, so when the small strings of beads were added the balls were protected, but the shanks were still worn by the constant touch of the fingers, as seen on bobbin *c*, which is so thin I hardly dare to use it. One sometimes sees bobbins with a new shank put into an old ball. Not all bobbins were equally used, or perhaps some were made of harder wood (bobbin *d*). Bone bobbins are stronger and heavier than wooden bobbins and therefore they were often made thinner and with a very little ball, sometimes like a disc, in the end

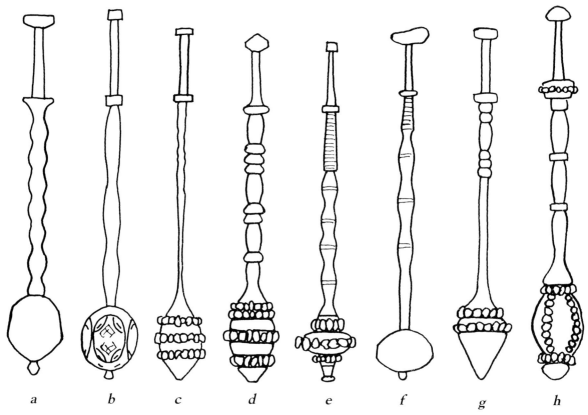

14a–n *Tønder bobbins, old and new*

(bobbin *e*). The bone bobbins are often thought to be ivory bobbins, but they are in fact made of bone from cow or horse, materials available in the area.

Some of the bobbins were given names. Bobbin *f* is made of bone with a dark wooden ball in the end. A bobbin like this is called 'solbær-øst'. It is impossible to translate directly: 'solbær' means 'blackcurrant', referring to the colour, and 'øst' means, in the local dialect, 'baby's bottom'—it is round and smooth! This bobbin has a big lump of sealing-wax on the top end. In the middle of the nineteenth century, when coarser thread came into use, the lacemakers enlarged the little disc with sealing-wax. Many bobbins still show traces of this wax though the big lump has gone

long ago. A bobbin with a fairly big, pointed cone in the end is called 'sugarloaf'. The cone is often dyed, mostly the same red as sealing-wax—perhaps sealing-wax was used—but a bluish-green is seen too. When the cone is dyed the top end of the bobbin is dyed too; it looks very pretty with all the tiny red spots shining up at you while you work (bobbin *g*).

Some bobbins are bigger and heavier and are meant for the gimp. There is the 'bride's bobbin' with a crown round the ball, associated with the peasant custom for a bride to wear a crown at her wedding (bobbin *h*). There is the 'mayor' with the big head (bobbin *i*). And there is the 'parson' with a ruff round the neck—the clergy of the Danish National Church wear a ruff with their gowns when serving in church (bobbin *j*).

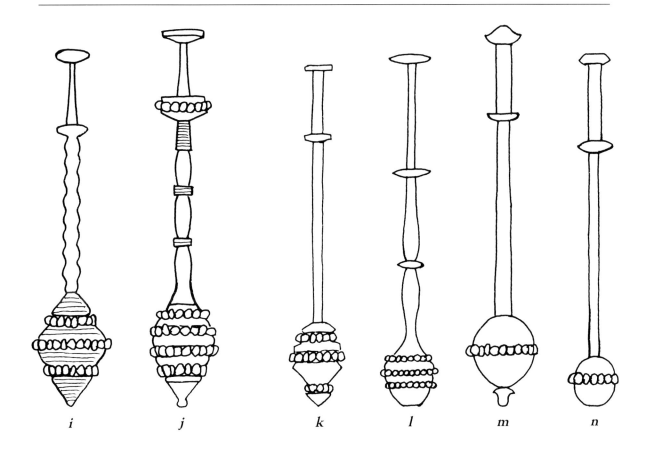

| *i* | *j* | *k* | *l* | *m* | *n* |

After 1864 many lacemakers decorated their bobbins with red and white beads as a silent demonstration against the German occupation.

The last four bobbins are newish, made as imitations of the old ones. The first one in this group (bobbin *k*) is good and works well together with the old ones. The second one (bobbin *l*) has overly large discs; they tend to cling to the neighbouring threads while working. The last two bobbins are good, bobbin *m* for the gimp and bobbin *n* for the thin thread.

No names of the old bobbin-makers are known. Local carpenters and people handy with a lathe made them for the lacemakers. When you look at the bobbins it is sometimes possible to see that two bobbins were made by the same person, but that is all we can say for sure at the moment.

It is difficult to find old Tønder bobbins for sale and they are expensive. Many good imitations are made today, so it is possible to get bobbins that look like the old ones. You can produce Tønder lace with the bobbins you are used to, if they are not too big and heavy. But I cannot deny that while working the samples for this book I did enjoy handling these original tiny works of art and admiring them, when I looked away from the lace for a moment. The thought of all the beautiful lace which these fragile old bobbins must have created has filled me with respect for those who used them to earn their humble living.

Dividers

The most simple dividers were made of a piece of brass wire, pointed at one end and with the other end bent into the shape of a trefoil. But, as human beings always like to use beautiful tools, the dividers were decorated in a similar way to the bobbins. The handle of *a* in diag. 15 is of turned wood and has strings of red and white beads. The little top is made of bone and is not original; probably it once had a top of nearly the same shape as the bottom. The other one (*b*) has a flat handle of bone with holes and incisions. The bottom is bulbous to allow room for the pin.

Pins

The pins must be stainless, either made of brass or some other rustproof material. For many years I have used insect pins with a diameter of $\frac{1}{72}$in. (0.35mm). But the pins used when the industry flourished were thicker, so now I have gone over to pins with a diameter of $\frac{1}{50}$in. (0.6mm). It makes the work easier and, in my opinion, the result is a more beautiful lace.

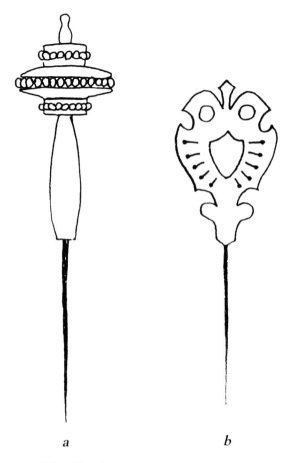

a   *b*

15a&b *Dividers*

Prickings

The old prickings were made of parchment and were not very long. There were no lines to show where to place the gimp or to indicate the progress of the pattern. The only help you had in finding your way through the hundreds and thousands of holes was two repeat lines, one near the top and one near the bottom of the parchment. The repeat line was just a fine scratch, made in order to help the lacemaker when she had reached the bottom of the parchment and was going to move the lace to the top, before she went on.

Today we use glazed cardboard for the prickings and, as most lacemakers use roller pillows, the pricking is made long enough to go round the roller. Usually the progress of the gimp is indicated with a line, at least on part of the pricking. It is important to draw this line very exactly, with a fine pen, as it may be difficult to see the holes if the line is cutting them. In a way I prefer to use a pricking without any lines; it makes the work more satisfying and you are forced to get better acquainted with the pattern.

—3—

Technique

In the same way as the style of Tønder lace was influenced by foreign lace types, the technique evolved until it was what we now consider the 'real' Tønder technique. Lille lace is the model for the technique as well as for the patterns, but, as mentioned above, Tønder lace became more individualized at the beginning of the nineteenth century. The background to the motifs is point ground in most of the patterns. The motifs are worked with cloth stitch or, less often, with half stitch, and you find honeycomb and some other decorative fillings, but there are not very many different fillings in Tønder lace. The figures are surrounded by a gimp, emphasizing the design and adding beautiful details. Tallies are scattered over the ground or form part of the motifs. The footside is mostly straight. The headside is nearly always worked with picots, not only because they look pretty, but also because the small springy picots protect the lace from wearing too quickly.

Tønder lace is always worked with the footside to the left and the headside to the right. For this book and in my lacemaking generally I tend to make the prickings for the laces of the Lille type on a rectangular grid, 0.9mm by 1.4mm, a grid that is suitable for most patterns of this type; other sizes and other proportions between length and breadth may be seen, even within the same pattern. Sometimes it is impossible to use a normal grid for the ground, because it will become too stiff; the ground has to be pricked in curved lines to follow the pattern. Some of my reconstructions are bigger than the old pieces, because the old ones were worked on a smaller scale, but I tried as far as possible to stick to the same scale for all patterns. This may have taken away some of the points of distinction you find in the old lace, but in this way I avoided having to prick the holes so close together that it is almost impossible to see where you are, and I have been able to stick to the same thread in all patterns of the Lille type. Before the middle of the nineteenth century nearly all lace was worked by the metre and, when used on, say, a scarf or a pocket-handkerchief, it was gathered in the corners. With the rectangular grid it is not easy to make a beautiful corner, so most of the patterns are without corners, as in the old days. All the corners in this book are made in accordance with the principles of the old techniques.

Thread

All samplers and most samples are worked with Brok Cotton Thread no. 140, and Bockens Knyppelgarn no. 35/3 for the gimp.

You may find two different gimps in a pattern, a thick one round the figures and a thin one as a passive in the footing and sometimes in the headside too. If lacemakers did not have suitable thread for a gimp, they might use seven or eight threads wound together on one bobbin. For many years linen has been considered the best for Tønder lace and I still think it is; it is more brilliant than cotton thread and stands the washing better. However, I have chosen this cotton thread for two reasons. First of all it is available, whereas it is difficult to get a really fine linen thread. Secondly the cotton thread is smoother than the linen, and it makes the pattern appear clearer in the samples. But you may use any thread you want, equivalent to those I have mentioned. The gimp may seem a little thick, but it has

to be so to emphasize the character of the pattern.

Stitches

The basic stitches—cloth stitch, half stitch, ground stitch, and honeycomb stitch, as well as tallies, picots, and the use of gimp—are shown in four samplers and in the first pieces of lace. Unless otherwise indicated, one thin line in the diagrams indicates one pair of threads, and a thick line indicates a single gimp thread. In some detail diagrams— tallies, footings and picots—one line indicates one thread. In a few cases a little dash across the line indicates a twist. The grounds and fillings are drawn in the same way throughout the book.

Samplers

First sampler
Cloth stitch and half stitch

Wind seven pairs with 140

These two fillings are used for the dense parts of the patterns. It may seem a little unnecessary to work these stitches in a sampler, but if you are not used to the thin thread it is a good way of practising.

First half of the sampler, cloth stitch
The top part (diag. 16) is worked with cloth stitch. Twist the worker pair twice before the outer passive pair on each side, work cloth stitch and twist and give the worker an extra twist, pin, cover the pin with cloth stitch and twist and an extra twist on the worker. This way of working the footside is not used very

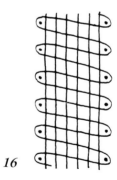

16

often, but it may still be seen. In the old days it was called the 'dotted footing'.

When cloth stitch is used as a filling the worker pair is twisted twice every time it passes round a pin. When beginning and

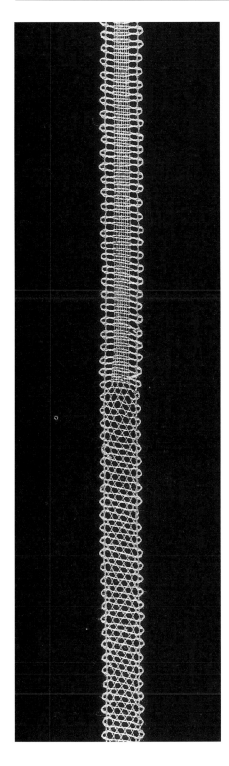

ending the cloth stitch filling with only two pairs, e.g. in a diamond, both pairs—the passive as well as the worker—are twisted twice. The result is that a little hole is formed, and that a very small piece of cloth stitch will appear as a little bunch of holes more than as a bit of cloth. But it is always—nearly always!—done that way in the old lace. Even if the lacemaker did not always make the correct number of twists in other parts of the lace, it looks as if here at least the rules were kept.

Second half of the sampler, half stitch
The bottom part (diag. 19) is worked with half stitch. Work the footings with cloth stitch and twists in the same way as in the cloth stitch part.

When half stitch is used as a filling, the worker pair gets an extra twist before covering the pin. You will find the half stitch filling used where the shape of the figure makes it difficult to get an even filling with cloth stitch, or, by alternating with cloth stitch, where two different effects are desired.

18

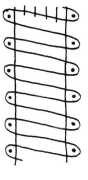

17 (*shown enlarged*)

19

Second sampler
Tallies

Wind eight pairs with 140

Work half stitch and twist (called honeycomb stitch below), pin, cover the pin with honeycomb stitch inside the passives of the footsides. For the footing, work cloth stitch and twist with the second (i.e. the passive) and the third pairs counted from outside, put up the pin between the two pairs. Now you have two pairs outside the pin. Work cloth stitch and twist with these two pairs and give the outer pair an extra twist. Put aside this pair and cover the pin with cloth stitch and twist and an extra twist on the worker. This footing was called the 'straight footing'.

The tallies are worked in four different ways, eight of each in this sampler. Common to all of them is that the weaver travels to and fro *about* nine times in a tally (some patterns demand a longer or a shorter tally).

In the detail diagrams for the tallies (diags 23*a-d*) one line means one thread. The diagrams show the progress of the threads in the different tallies, but not the actual length of the tally. (The small drawings show how the tallies are drawn in the pattern diagrams.)

21

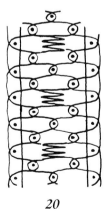

20

22 (shown enlarged)

First tally

This tally (23a) is worked in the way mostly used today with the middle thread across the tally. The weaver begins and ends in opposite corners. This tally has a tendency to slant a little.

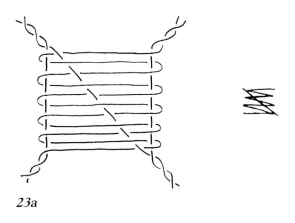

23a

Second tally

This tally (23b) is worked as most tallies were in the old lace, with the middle thread running along the left side. The weaver begins and ends on the right side. This tally has a tendency to become a little fan-shaped.

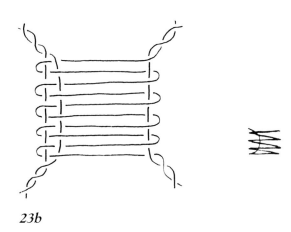

23b

Third and fourth tallies

Refer to diags 23c and d.

These tallies are worked on the same principles, but with the weaver going twice

round the passives in the sides. It takes a little more time, but it is easier to avoid pulling the weaver too hard, and in this way it becomes easier to give the tally a beautiful shape.

Sometimes the tallies are reversed, and you may find different ways of working the tallies in the same piece of lace. The way I have worked the tallies in the patterns can be seen in the diagrams, but it is not important to use the same method as me. It is more important to find the method that gives you the best result and stick to that.

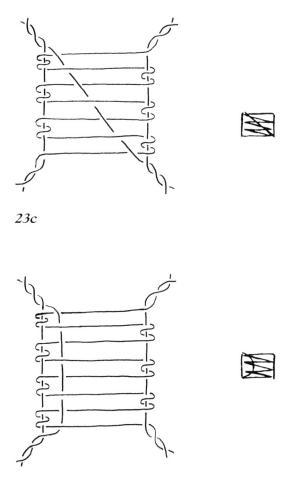

23c

23d

Third sampler
Point ground, tallies, and three different footings

Wind 16 pairs with 140

Point ground (called 'ground' below) is worked with half stitch and two twists: *the pins are never covered*. Work the ground in diagonal lines to the right or left, as is most convenient. Try to get a rhythm working in your fingers when working the ground; it makes it easier to remember not to cover the pins and to make a beautiful ground.

With very few exceptions you find a straight footside in Tønder lace, but it is worked in different ways. Today most lacemakers use the so-called 'Cumberland footing', as shown in the top part of the sampler. In the old lace the footsides are worked differently, with a good deal of variation, mostly in the choice and use of the passives. Two variations are shown in this sampler; others will appear in the following patterns. I have generally used the old footing as being that which suits the old patterns best.

Top section
In the top section (27a) you work ground throughout, and so you can get used to it. The footsides are worked with Cumberland footing. There are two passive pairs in the footing. Work the ground stitch next to the passive pairs with the fourth and fifth pairs, counted from outside, and put up the catch pin between the third and fourth pairs. Cloth stitch the fourth pair through the two passive pairs, twist twice or perhaps three times, put up the foot pin inside two pairs, and work a cloth stitch and two or three twists outside the pin. Now you have a new worker pair.

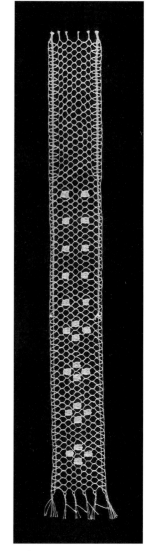

25

24

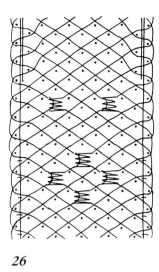

26

with three threads, the latter at the outside. This way of putting together the threads of the passive pair was very common. Work a cloth stitch and three twists—sometimes only one or two twists—next to the passive pair, with the third and fourth pairs, counted from outside, and put up the pin *under* the stitch. Do not cover the pin as if the stitch is a ground stitch. Cloth stitch the third pair through the passive pair and work the foot pin as explained above.

Put aside the outer pair, cloth stitch through the passive pairs with the new worker pair, and continue in the ground. Very often a half stitch is used instead of a cloth stitch outside the outer pin, but I prefer cloth stitch, because it gives a firmer footside.

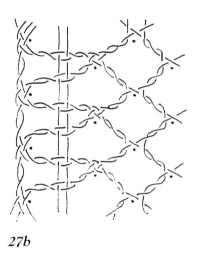

27b

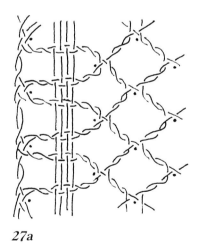

27a

Middle section
In the middle section (27b) the footsides are worked with only one passive pair, consisting of one bobbin with a single thread and one

In this part you work the tallies one by one, as is done in many patterns to add life to the ground. Work ground as far as possible to both sides of the tally. I have used the second tally (diag. 23b) so the weaver is on the right-hand side when the tally is finished. For that reason you have to work the left side of the ground before the right-hand side, after you have worked the tally. Work the left tally first. When it is finished, support the weaver, twist the pair in the bottom left-hand corner twice, work a ground stitch, put up the pin in the corner of the tally, and continue in a diagonal line to the left footside. Work the ground stitch in the bottom right-hand corner of the tally. You will get the best result if the weaver and the right-hand passive are twisted twice, so the passive from the tally is the thread that goes straight through the ground to the right footside. As you cannot go on to the right-hand side before the right tally is finished, you have to continue in a diagonal line to the left footside, being careful not to pull the weaver. Work the right tally in the same way, but this time you can work from the bottom left-hand corner to the left side, as above, and from the bottom right-hand corner to the right footside, before working the ground stitch beneath the tally. It is always a good idea to work as much as possible with the passive threads from the tally before using the weaver again.

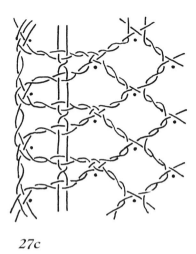

27c

Lower section

The footsides in the third part (27c) are worked with only one passive pair, consisting of two single threads. The procedure is almost the same as in the middle section except that the passive pair is twisted once after the cloth stitch that brings the worker pair from outside the passive pair into the ground. The result is that the workers are lying a little more apart than without the twist, and the connection between footing and ground is more attractive.

In this part four tallies form a group as they often do, as a part of the pattern or to break the monotony of the ground. I have used the same tally as above (diag. 23b). Work ground as far as possible to both sides of the group. Work the top tally and finish with a ground stitch in the bottom left-hand corner, in the bottom right-hand corner and in the middle beneath the tally. Go on with the left tally and, when it is finished, work ground from the bottom left-hand corner to the left footside, and from the bottom right-hand corner to the left footside. Work the right tally and finish with a ground stitch in the bottom left-hand corner, and work ground from the bottom right-hand corner to the right footside, and from the pin beneath the tally to the right footside. Go on with the bottom tally and work ground from the bottom left-hand corner to the left footside and from the bottom right-hand corner to the right footside. Work ground until next group of tallies.

Fourth sampler
Two fillings: honeycomb and elder blossom

Wind 18 pairs with 140

Top section: honeycomb

Honeycomb is, like cloth stitch, used in most patterns. The footing is worked with cloth stitch and three twists, no twists on the passive pair. Honeycomb is usually worked with honeycomb stitch, pin, honeycomb stitch. Wherever possible, work honeycomb in diagonal rows, alternating a continuous row with a gap row. The continuous row has to be worked from the hole furthest away from you to the hole nearest to you, whereas the gap row may be worked from the nearest hole to the furthest one in the row: take two pairs and work the first pin; put aside both pairs, take the next two pairs and work the second pin; put away both pairs etc. In this way you avoid moving the bobbins from one side of the pillow to the other more than is strictly necessary.

In the sides of the honeycomb filling the little hole round the pin is very often slightly oblong from one side to the other, as you can see in the first half of the honeycomb. To avoid that the old lacemakers worked a cloth stitch and two twists, pin, and covered the pin with a honeycomb stitch as usual. I have worked in this way in the second half of the honeycomb at the pins next to the passives in the footings. It makes the threads fit closely round the pin. The stitch is mostly worked in this way just inside the gimp on the vertical sides of a figure, where the worker pair from a cloth stitch travels into a honeycomb filling; and in the top and bottom of the small hexagons in the honeycomb. But I have seen lace where I could not find any system at all in the use of this technique.

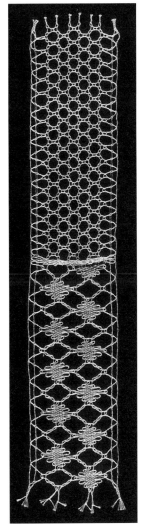

28

29

Lower section: elder blossom

The elder blossom is a quite open filling; it does not demand as many pairs as the honeycomb, so you have to take away four pairs and work with only 14.

The footings are worked with cloth stitch and a good many twists on the worker pairs as well as on the passive pairs, in order to make it fairly firm. The filling consists of cloth-stitch diamonds, held together by small pin chains. *Note* that at two pins before the middle no new passive pairs enter the cloth stitch; and in the same way, no passive pairs leave the cloth stitch at the corresponding pins after the middle. It is important to remember the twists at these pins and perhaps to make an extra one. The pin chains are worked with cloth stitch and twists. I have used one twist round the two pins in the chain, and two twists where the pairs are entering the diamond. But you may find the same filling with two or even three twists after every cloth stitch. Sometimes the worker in the diamond is twisted twice just before and after the cloth stitch round the outer pins, half-way through the diamond. This filling is used in rather big figures.

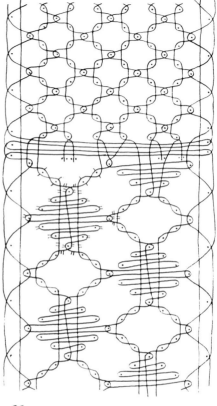

30

— 4 —
Three patterns used as samplers

Pattern 1:
Narrow insertion

Wind 16 pairs with 140; plus two pairs: one bobbin with 140 and one with 35/2; and another pair with 35/3

I use this insertion to explain *how to use the gimp*. When putting in the gimp you must pay attention to the twists before and after the gimp. In *ground* there are only two twists before and after the gimp, i.e. you have to take away one twist, where the gimp is going to pass through a pair. In *honeycomb* you may see one or two twists before and after the gimp, according to the nature of the pattern. When the gimp surrounds a *cloth stitch* figure, only one twist is used where the gimp is worked diagonally, and no twists at all where the gimp is horizontal or vertical and is therefore lying parallel with either the worker pair or the passives.

If two gimps are following each other through some pairs, they may be worked in different ways. The gimps may pass together through the threads, so they are lying in the same 'shed'; the two threads of a pair may change places between the gimps; or you may twist the threads between the gimps, all in accordance with the pattern. Usually the gimps are crossed right over left, but you

may cross left over right. However, the gimps should cross in the same direction throughout the whole lace to create a pretty effect. These are the main rules. If the pattern is open or the thread is a little thin in proportion to the pricking, use more twists and, on the other hand, if the pattern is dense or the thread a little thick, use fewer twists. Your own way of handling the bobbins and the thread matters a good deal too. With a little practice it is possible to form the lines of the gimp by means of the number of twists.

Proceed as follows when you pass a gimp through a pair: if the number of twists is correct, lift up the *right* bobbin of the pair, pass the gimp under this thread and over the other one, from one side of the pair to the other. Lay down the bobbin in your hand to the left of the bobbin on the pillow and make the desired number of twists. If you need to take away one twist, you do not have to do this in a separate movement; lift up the *left* bobbin of the pair, pass the gimp under this thread and over the other one, and lay down the bobbin in your hand to the left of the bobbin on the pillow and make the twists. Pull the gimp carefully to avoid an uneven line.

This pattern is worked with one twist before and one after the gimp and there is a twist

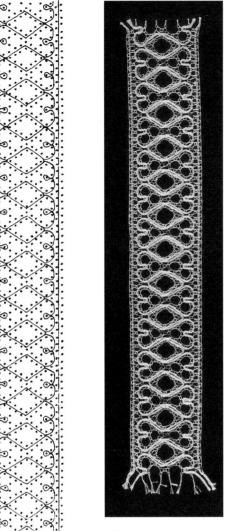

31

32

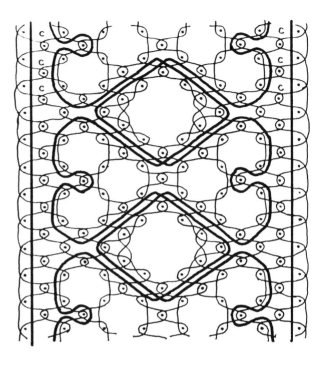

33

between the gimps, where they follow each other. The odd pairs are used as passives in the footings, with the gimp at the outer side. They are worked with cloth stitch as normal pairs and with two twists on the worker pair on either side of the passive pair. Work the catch pin with cloth stitch and two twists, pin, cover the pin with honeycomb stitch; the letter *c* over the stitch in the diagram indicates where it is done. Work honeycomb stitch inside the diamond shape: follow the lines in the diagram and work honeycomb stitch every time two lines cross. A ring like this may be worked in other ways, especially a large ring which may have more threads inside the gimp, but the principle in all these rings is to include all pairs inside the gimp in the net along the sides.

Pattern 2:
Cock's eye

Wind 12 pairs with 140, one bobbin with 35/3

I use this lace to explain *how to work the headside with picots and scallops.*

Picots

First picot
Refer to diags 34a–d.

Pass the worker pair which is meant for the picot round the gimp, and cloth stitch through the passive pairs of the headside, perhaps with a twist between the gimp and the passives. Twist the worker pair nine

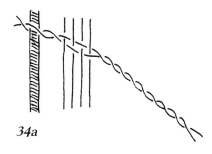

34a

times (*a*). Take up the pair between the fingers of your left hand and turn your hand round so the palm is facing you. Take a pin in your right hand and pass it from below the outer thread; turn it towards yourself, and put it into the hole (*b*). Pass the other thread

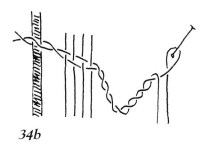

34b

the same way round the pin and back to its place, coax the threads little by little until the twists are lying all the way round the pin; you may sometimes hear a little click when it happens. The two threads from the bobbins should now be either side of the twisted part

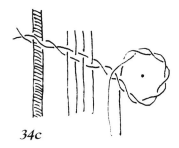

34c

(*c*). Twist the worker pair twice, cloth stitch through the passive pairs, pass round the gimp, and go on with the lace (*d*).

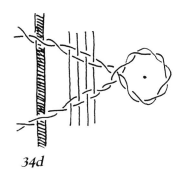

34d

Second picot
Refer to diags 35a and b.

Pass the worker pair round the gimp and cloth stitch through the passive pairs until the last pair. Twist and work cloth stitch and twist with the outer passive pair. Twist the worker pair six to eight times. Take up the pair with your left hand, pass a pin with your right hand, from underneath both threads, turn it away from yourself, and put it into the hole. Both threads should be round the

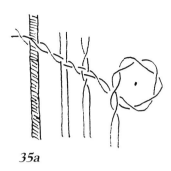

35a

pin with the free ends on the top (*a*). Take one of the bobbins in your right hand and pass the thread backwards round the pin to push all the twists together, and then pass it forward again to its place; keep the other thread taut all the time. Work a cloth stitch and twist with the worker pair and the outer passive pair, pull the stitch very carefully up to the picot, cloth stitch through the passive pairs, pass round the gimp, and go on with the lace (*b*). You may leave out the twist on the worker pair between the outer passive pair and the rest of the passive pairs, but the twist on the *outer* passive pair is necessary to hold the picot in the right position.

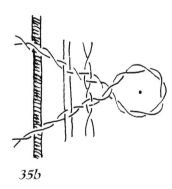

35b

Scallops

Only in the top of a scallop or along a straight headside can you take the picot pair from inside the gimp, work the picot, and return to the pattern. At the start of a scallop you take a pair from the passive pairs, work the picot, and pass the pair through the passive pairs to join the pattern. And at the end of a scallop you take a pair from the pattern, pass it through the passive pairs, work the picot, and leave the pair among the passive pairs. There are two basic methods.

First method
Refer to diag. 36*a*.

Take the second pair from the right, cloth stitch with the outer passive pair, work the picot, cloth stitch through all passive pairs, and pass the pair round the gimp to take part in the pattern. Continue in this way, taking the second pair from the right for the picot each time, until all pairs necessary to the pattern have been passed inside the gimp.

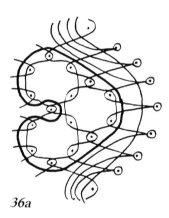

36a

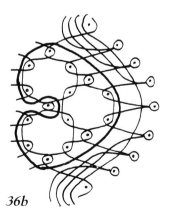

36b

After you have worked the top of the scallop pass a pair round the gimp, cloth stitch through the passive pairs, work the picot, cloth stitch with the outer passive pair, and leave the pair as the second from the right.

At the top of the scallop one pair may pass to and fro between the picots and the interior of the lace several times. If so, use enough passive pairs to have two of them left in the top to support the picots; one pair is not enough unless, as in the diagram, the picot pair is only passing in and out twice.

Second method
Refer to diag. 36b.

Take the passive pair next to the gimp, cloth stitch through all the passive pairs, work the

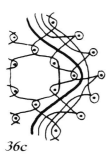

36c

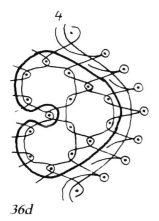

36d

picot, cloth stitch through all the passive pairs, and pass the pair round the gimp. Go on like this, each time taking the pair next to the gimp for the picot. The top of the scallop is worked as described before. After the top pass a pair round the gimp, cloth stitch through all the passive pairs, work the picot, cloth stitch through all the passive pairs, and leave the pair next to the gimp. In this way you get a firmer headside.

In a lace with many passive pairs in the headside any pair from these may be used for a picot. Sometimes, some of the passives are gathered in a bunch and passed between the threads of the worker pair like a gimp, and the worker pair will only cloth stitch through one or two outer pairs. One gimp or a pair of gimps, usually a little thinner than the gimps in the pattern, may be used as passives. Sometimes you will need more pairs for picots than you can get from the pattern. If so, take one of the passive pairs, cloth stitch with the outer pair or pairs, work the picot, and pass the pair back to its place among the passives. Or it may be done as shown in diag. 36c, where two pairs are changed about.

At the *nook pin* (the pin between each scallop repeat) you will not find a picot in Tønder lace. Pass the worker pair round the gimp and cloth stitch through all the passive pairs, twist twice outside the nook pin, and pass the worker pair back again, ready to enter the pattern. This is the simplest method but in some patterns the arrangement around the nook pin is different. It is not always easy to figure out why, but I have tried to be as faithful to the old patterns as possible.

As it is rather difficult and sometimes impossible to show all the passive pairs in the diagrams, especially round the nook pin, I have drawn most of the diagrams like diag. 36d where the number of passive pairs at the nook pin is given by means of a figure.

In some of the patterns I have described the way I have worked the scallops and the footing as well, which in most cases is as they were in the piece of lace I was reconstructing. But if you prefer to use one of the other methods, this is perfectly satisfactory.

In this pattern the footing is worked with cloth stitch through the passive pairs and cloth stitch and three twists outside the foot pin. In the corner the foot pin and the pin next to it are used twice. Work as usual for the first time and when you come to the pin for the second time, remove the pin and use it again for the new stitch in the same hole. The rest of the lace is worked with honeycomb stitch and, as this will be a little loose, there are two twists on both sides of the gimp, even between the gimp and the headside passives. There are three passive pairs at each nook pin in order to have two of them left in the top of the scallop. The first type of picot is used in this pattern.

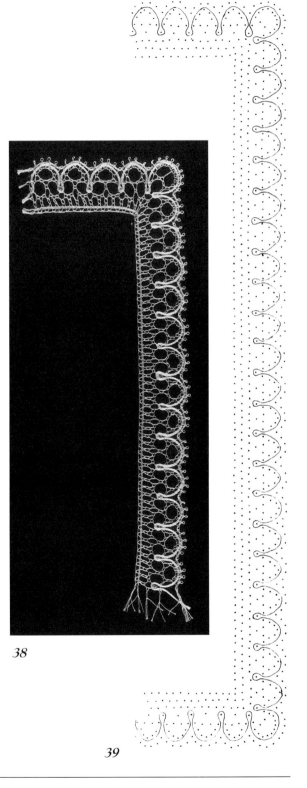

38

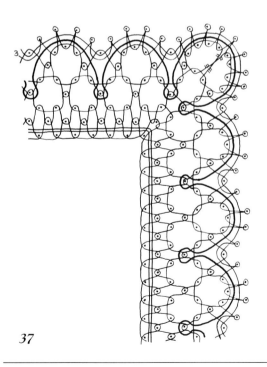

37

39

46

Pattern 3:
Tiny cock's eye

Wind six pairs with 140, one bobbin with 35/3

Perhaps this little piece of lace looks more
like a cock's eye than the pattern above. I
include it because I think it is suitable for
doll's clothes. The footing is worked with
cloth stitch and one, two or three twists as
indicated in the diagram. The rest of the lace
is worked with honeycomb stitch.

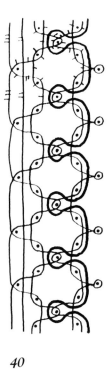

40

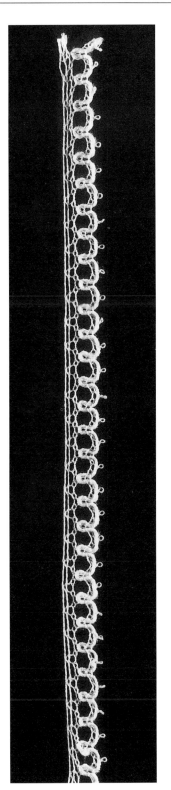

41   *(shown enlarged)*

42

—5—

Eight easy patterns

Pattern 4:
The eye and the hook

Wind 16 pairs with 140, one bobbin with 35/3

These two patterns were made on the same pricking. Nowadays one often uses two different prickings, but I find it more interesting to use only one and work two variations.

For many years this pattern was the most common one used for children's clothes. The footing is worked with cloth stitch and two twists on the worker pair, the passive pair has one twist every second time. The ground is worked in the old way at the catch pin. The 'heart' in the eye and the 'diamond' in the hook are worked with honeycomb but in the diamond you do not use the hole with the ring around. The big ring in the eye is worked according to the same principles as explained for Pattern 1, with a honeycomb stitch every time two pairs cross each other. I have tried two variations as shown in the diagram; there is little difference to be seen in the finished lace.

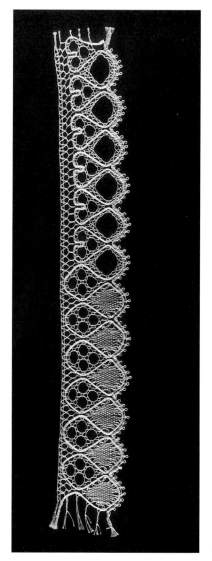

43

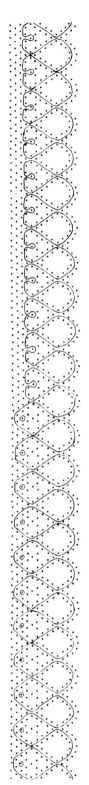

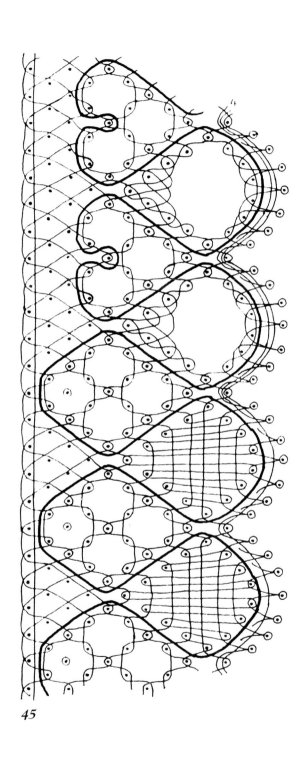

44

45

49

Pattern 5:
Tallies and gimp

Wind 16 pairs with 140, one pair: one bobbin with one thread and one bobbin with three threads 140, one bobbin with 35/3

I think it is fascinating to have a pattern composed of only a gimp and some tallies, hence its title. The odd pair is used as a passive pair in the footing, with three threads at the outside. The loops made with the gimp are found in many patterns, sometimes so numerous that they form a sort of ribbon (*see* Pattern 45). It may seem a little tricky to work in the beginning, but the following explanation should help you. The ground is quite regular between the loops. When the loops are moving *to the left*, pass the gimp to the left through four pairs and to the right through three pairs. When the loops are

moving *to the right*, pass the gimp to the right through four pairs and to the left through three pairs. When the loops are moving *vertically*, pass the gimp through three pairs every time. As the tallies are an important part of the pattern, I have chosen the tally from diag. 23d, because it is an easy one to make beautifully. In this lace it is reversed—I tried to work it both ways, but this way proved the best. Work the group of four tallies in this order: top, right, left, then bottom; like this it is easy to secure the passives before going on with the weaver in the ground. The method of progressing round the nook pin is somewhat unusual, as the outer passive pair is replaced with another one. The way to work the pairs round the nook pin is shown in the detail diag. 47. The first type of picot is used.

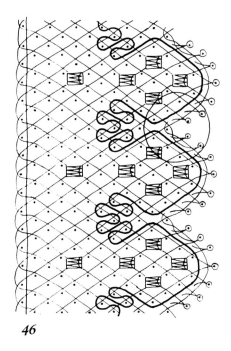

46

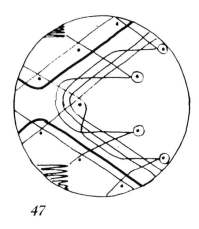

47

![Lace sample 48 and pattern diagram 48a](# "image-left")

48

48a

Pattern 6:
Ellen

Wind 22 pairs with 140, one pair with 35/3

In about 1900 a lacemaker called Ellen worked this pattern, which has been given her name. It belongs to the same family as 'The eye and the hook', but the pattern has been worked out a little more. One passive pair is used in the footing, worked with cloth

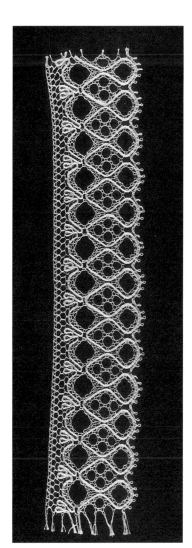

49

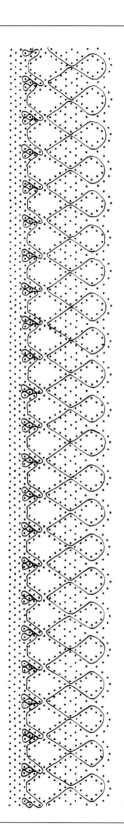

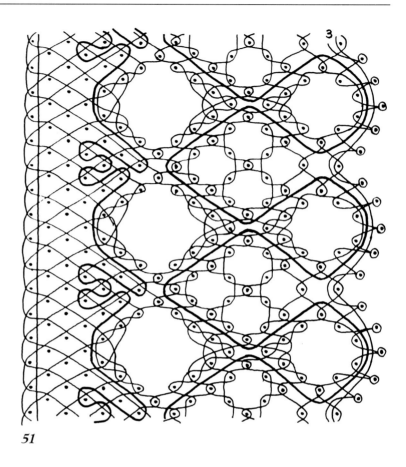

51

50

stitch. Work the gimp loops as explained in Pattern 5. The net inside the gimp is made a little differently from that in 'The eye', but the principle is the same: use all the pairs inside the gimp along the sides of the ring to get a rather large hole in the middle. *Note*: only one pair travels in and out to all the picots, so you must have two passive pairs along the headside, i.e. three passive pairs in the nook.

Pattern 7:
Toadstool

Wind 15 pairs with 140, one pair with 35/3

I have used the Cumberland footing in this lace, but with only one passive pair. It is worked with cloth stitch and a twist every second time. The loops of the gimp are worked as in 'Tallies and gimp', the only difference being the honeycomb stitch in the middle. Honeycomb stitches are used in the scallop and in the ring. In the scallops I have taken the pair next to the gimp in each case to work the picots and used the first type of picot.

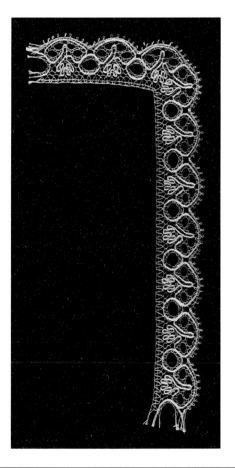

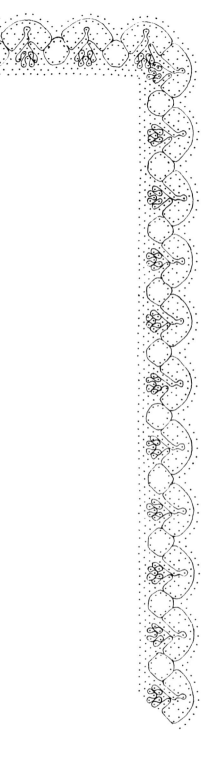

52

53

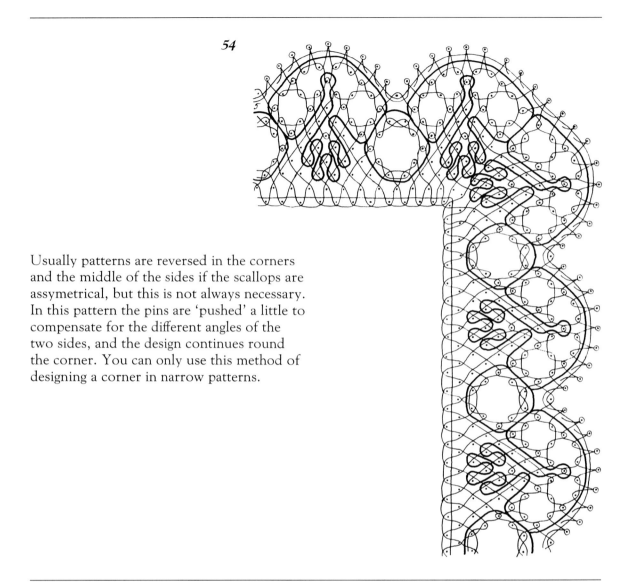

Usually patterns are reversed in the corners and the middle of the sides if the scallops are assymetrical, but this is not always necessary. In this pattern the pins are 'pushed' a little to compensate for the different angles of the two sides, and the design continues round the corner. You can only use this method of designing a corner in narrow patterns.

Pattern 8:
Ram's horn

Wind 14 pairs with 140, one pair: one bobbin with one thread and one bobbin with two threads 140, one pair with 35/3

The pattern reminded me of a ram's horn, so I gave it this name. The odd pair is used as a passive pair in the footing, with two threads at the outside. The loops of the gimp are worked in the same way as in 'Tallies and gimp', only with more vertical loops. Where the pairs pass through each other without pins to the right of the loops, they are worked with cloth stitch, with no twists except for those around the gimps. Work cloth stitch and twist, where two pairs are crossing between the honeycomb ring and the gimp; this way of working the threads inside the gimps which surround a honeycomb ring, is often used (*see* Patterns 34, 35 and 36). Although the scallops look identical they are worked in two different ways, the second being a reflection of the first. *Note*: in every second nook one passive pair is taken together with the gimp to the inner nook pin whereas in the other nooks all passives remain just inside the nook pin, while the gimps are twisted round each other without a pin.

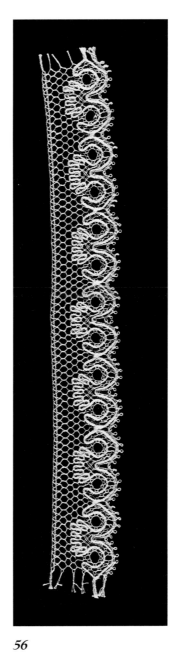

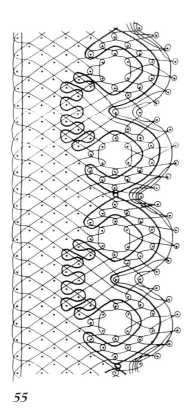

55

56

57

Pattern 9:
Little heart of Denmark

Wind ten pairs with 140, one bobbin with 35/2, one bobbin with 35/3 or wind 11 pairs with 140, one bobbin with 35/3

In the straight sample (60*a*), the thin gimp is used as a passive in the footing. The stitch without a pin between the hearts and their curves is a cloth stitch and two twists. The gimp loops are held together with honeycomb stitches, and ground is worked in the space inside the loops. The half stitch in the heart may be replaced by cloth stitch, but this does not look as graceful as the half stitch.

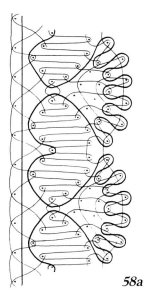

58a

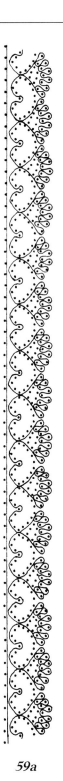

59a

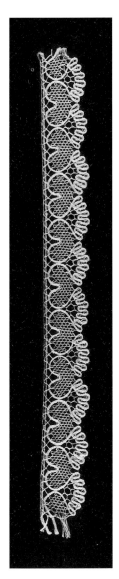

60a

The passive gimp in the footing may be replaced by a pair of threads as it is done in the corner (60*b*), and in the curved lace (60*c*). The passive pair is worked with cloth stitch and two twists everywhere. *Note:* in these two samples the outer pairs in the headside are worked differently from those in the straight sample, when they come to the nook

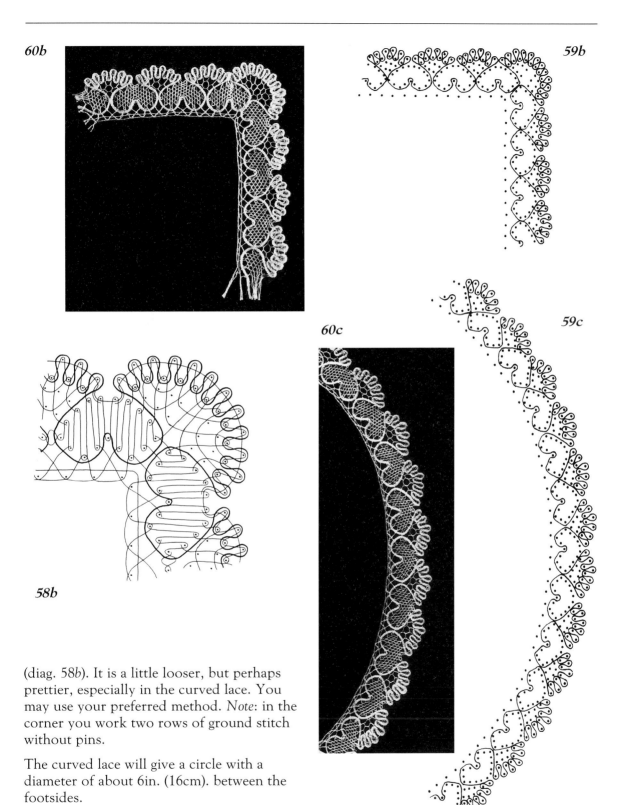

60b

59b

60c

59c

58b

(diag. 58*b*). It is a little looser, but perhaps prettier, especially in the curved lace. You may use your preferred method. *Note*: in the corner you work two rows of ground stitch without pins.

The curved lace will give a circle with a diameter of about 6in. (16cm). between the footsides.

Pattern 10:
Little Kirsten

Wind 18 pairs with 140, one pair with 35/3 for the insertion (a). Wind 17 pairs with 140, one pair with 35/3 for the lace (b)

This insertion was one of the first Tønder patterns I ever worked. As I am very fond of it, I was pleased when recently I found the corresponding lace among some old samples.

The footsides are worked with Cumberland footing, with one passive pair worked with cloth stitch. The Cumberland footing suggests that the pattern is not very old and must be a simplification of Pattern 11. The

61a

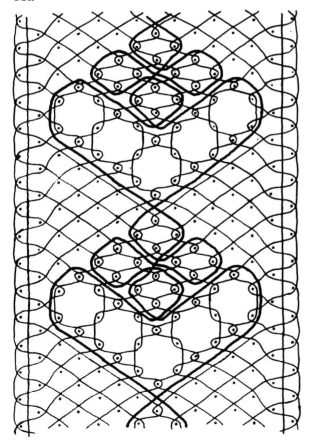

62a

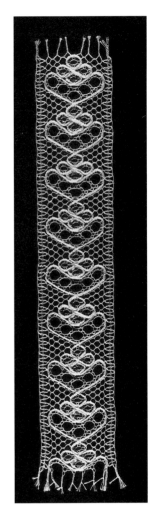

63a

heart-shaped figure and the four-pin buds are worked with honeycomb stitches, surrounded by gimps. Where the four-pin buds are put together in groups of four as in this pattern, one gimp travels quite straight from top to bottom while the other gimp travels round the right and left bud. By this method you avoid a hole in the middle of the group. The passive pair nearest the gimp is used for each picot. *Note*: two pairs are crossed inside the nook pin.

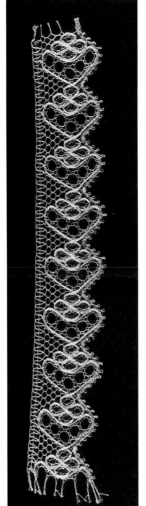

63b

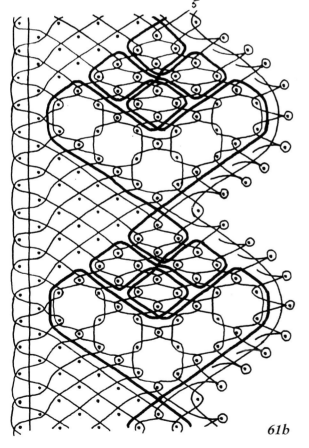

61b

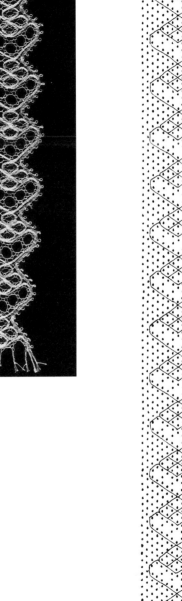

62b

Pattern 11:
Double Little Kirsten

Wind 33 pairs with 140, four pairs with 35/3

This pattern is taken from a lace merchant's sample book of 1820. If you have made the previous pattern, the middle of this will cause no difficulties.

A new feature is the footing with blocks. Work cloth stitch and twist outside the blocks, where you have the dotted footing. If you want the straight footing, add one pair in

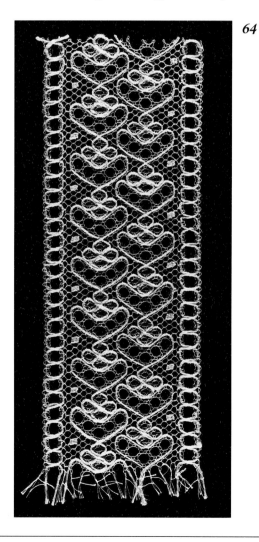

64

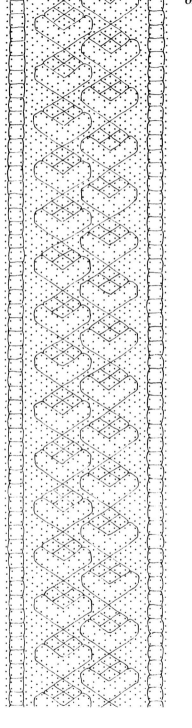

65

each side and work in the usual way with
cloth stitch and two twists outside the pin.
Work the four pins in the blocks with
honeycomb stitch. Work the ground pins
next to the blocks with cloth stitch and two
or three twists.

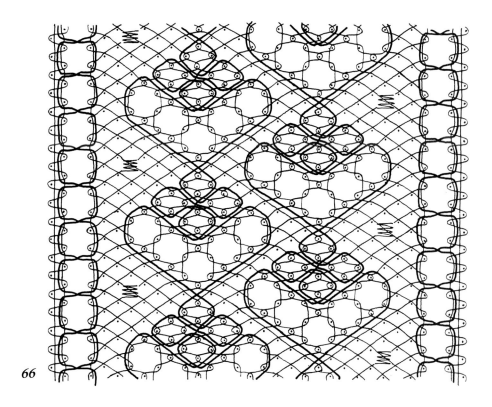

66

$-6-$
Nine more elaborate patterns

Pattern 12:
Lace with starfish I

Wind 11 pairs with 140, one bobbin with 35/2, one pair with 35/3. Wind one extra pair with 140 and one with 35/3 for the corner

Use the thin gimp as a passive in the footing and work the catch pin in the traditional way. The starfish may be a little tricky. Follow the path of the threads as shown in the diagram; work ground stitch in the end of all six arms and cloth stitch in the rest of the figure, without giving the worker pair any twists. It makes it easier if you work as much as possible outside the starfish every time a pair has passed round the gimp to the ground; in this way the pairs will always be ready to enter the starfish when you need them. The first type of picot is used, but nevertheless all passive pairs in the headside are twisted. The pair coming from the upper right arm, and the pair coming from the picot (x) have to be worked with cloth stitch and two twists, pin at (y), honeycomb stitch to make the stitch fit round the pin.

To work the corner: hang the extra pair round the nook pin before the corner scallop, between the worker pair and the passive pair, and work cloth stitch with the pair to the left. Pass the worker through all

four passive pairs, remove the pin so the loop of the new pair is free, replace the pin between the worker pair and the passive pairs and continue as usual. Put a pin into the first honeycomb hole in the corner, hang the extra gimp pair round it, and pass the threads round the gimp. Work a honeycomb stitch, remove the pin and replace it under the stitch, cover the pin with a honeycomb stitch. Work cloth stitch and two twists between the starfish and the ring in the corner. *Note*: the new pair in the headside is

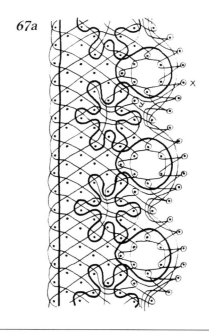

67a

used as a passive pair until needed for the third picot without being used inside the gimp. When you discard the gimp pair both gimps will overlap each other as you pass them through the pairs from the last honeycomb stitch in the corner and lay them at the back of the pillow. When you have finished the scallop and are sure the gimps are pulled sufficiently taut you may cut them off. When discarding the extra pair from the passive pairs in the headside, take away the third and fifth threads counting from the left side of the passive pairs. Later on, when the pins are removed, all discarded threads can be cut off close to the lace.

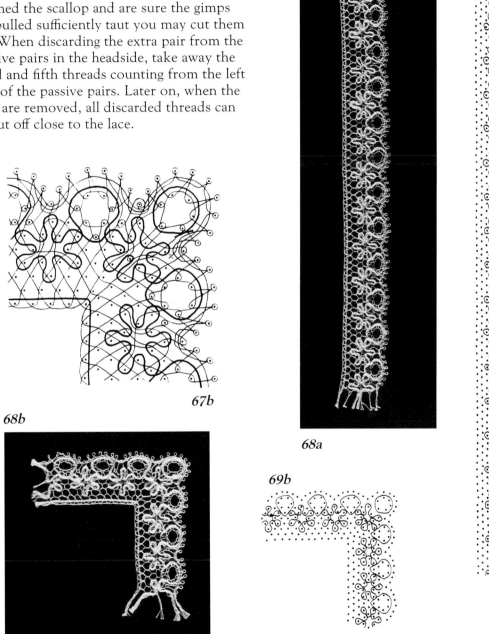

67b

68b

68a

69b

69a

Pattern 13:
Lace with starfish II

Wind 26 pairs with 140, two pairs: one bobbin with 140 and one with 35/3, one pair and two single bobbins with 35/3

The odd pairs are used as a passive pair in the footing and as the outer pair in the headside, both with the gimp at the outer side. Most of this pattern is easy, as it consists of ground and honeycomb, separated by a gimp, and the scallop is quite regular. *Note*: two pairs are crossed with a cloth stitch in the nook between the scallops. This is done rather often, sometimes with several pairs, probably to avoid a gap inside the passives.

The starfish may cause you some problems. If you have worked Pattern 12, you may choose to work the starfish in the same way. I worked this one a little differently to follow the old sample. Hang the gimp pair on a pin in the upper left arm, pass it through the two pairs from the sides, work a cloth stitch, remove the pin and replace it under the cloth stitch. Follow the diagram and work cloth stitch in the top and bottom arms and ground stitch in the side arms and in the nooks. Work cloth stitch in the middle with a twist on the worker pair inside the gimp. The gimps are discarded in the bottom left-hand arm. Pass both gimps through both

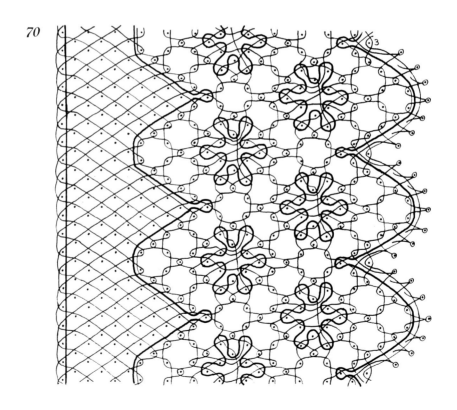

70

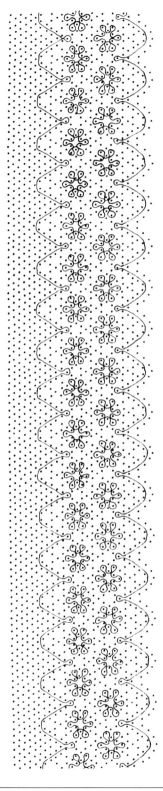

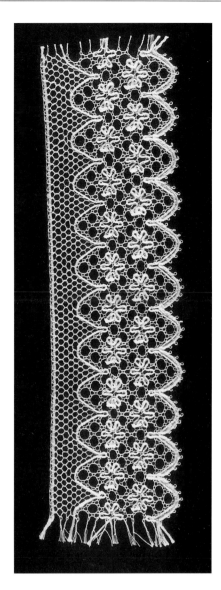

pairs, overlapping each other, and put them away to the back of the pillow. It makes it easier if you work as much honeycomb to the sides of the starfish as possible every time a pair leaves the starfish. When you come to the next starfish, cut off the gimps a little above the pin heads, tie them together, and unwind one bobbin just a little, so that the knot will not be seen in the lace. When you have removed the lace, you can cut off the gimp ends very close to the work.

Pattern 14:
Lace with spiders

Wind 14 pairs with 140, one pair: one bobbin with 140 and one with 35/2, one pair with 35/3

You will rarely see a spider in Tønder lace from this period. When they appear, they are always small, and used as a decorative touch, say in a calyx in a flower pattern or, as here, in a ring of honeycomb stitches.

The odd pair is used as a passive pair in the footing, with the gimp thread at the outer side. Work honeycomb stitch in the gimp loops and in the ring, with two twists before and after the gimp. The second type of picot is used, and only the passive pair is twisted.

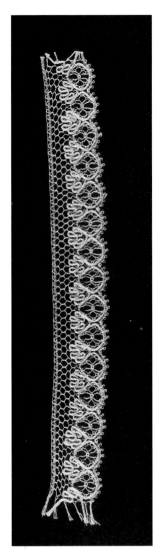

74

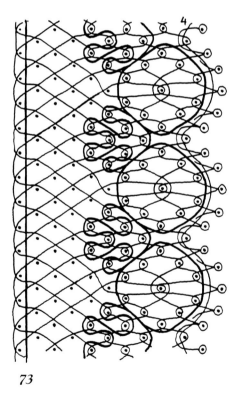

73

75

Pattern 15:
Lace with spiders and a flower

Wind 22 pairs with 140, one pair: one bobbin with one thread and one with three threads 140, one bobbin with 35/2, two pairs with 35/3

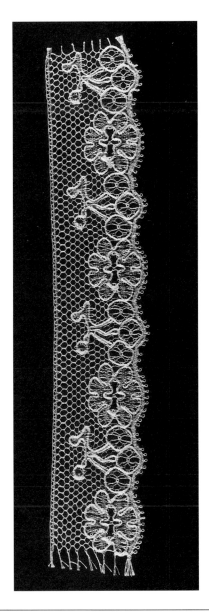

76

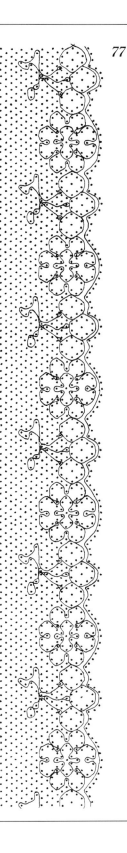

77

The odd pair is used as a passive pair in the footing, with three threads at the outer side. The bobbin with the thin gimp is used as the outer passive thread in the headside, together with two pairs of fine thread. Work cloth stitch in the stem and the little leaf. Work cloth stitch and two twists, pin, honeycomb stitch in the top and bottom of the little bud. Work cloth stitch in the sides of the bud and twist the worker pair twice round the pin outside the gimp. In the thin stems the pairs change places between the gimps, but in the ends at the support pin there is an extra twist in the first and third stems and a ground stitch in the second.

The flower is worked entirely in cloth stitch. In the nooks between the petals the threads are twisted to separate the gimps. The pairs coming from the picots are not enough to fill up the right petal of the flower, so you have to take an extra pair out of the headside passives to join the pattern. Take the passive pair next to the gimp, twist once, pass it round the gimp, and use it as a worker pair in the petal.

Two different scallops used alternately as seen in this pattern are often found in Tønder lace, as well as one scallop divided into small scallops. It is mostly found like this in the floral patterns, as you can see in Patterns 29, 32, 34 and others.

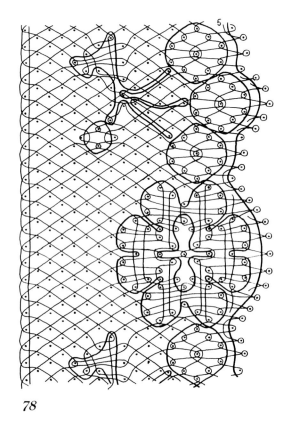

78

Pattern 16:
Slanting leaf I

Wind 25 pairs with 140, two pairs and one bobbin with 35/3

Slanting leaf is not one pattern only, but a whole group. The common feature is a rather big, slanting leaf, worked with cloth stitch and surrounded by a gimp. Also frequently found in these patterns is a line of rings along the footside and a scallop filled with honeycomb.

The footing has one normal pair, twisted after each stitch. The ground between the

footing and the rings may be worked entirely
with cloth stitch and three twists or, as in my
sample, with cloth stitch and three twists at
the catch pin, and ground stitch for the rest.
Where the gimps lie together on the long
side of the leaf the threads are twisted
between them, whereas there are no twists
between the gimps on the other side. *Note:*
the number of honeycomb rings along the
footside does not correspond to the rest of
the pattern, so the repeat is three scallops
long.

79

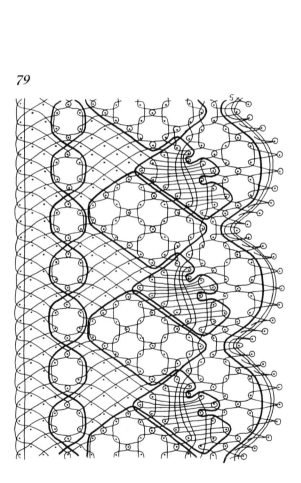

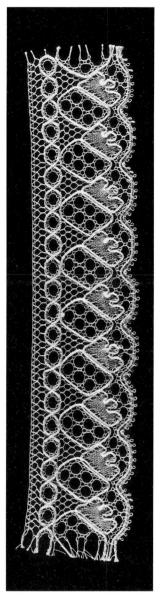

80

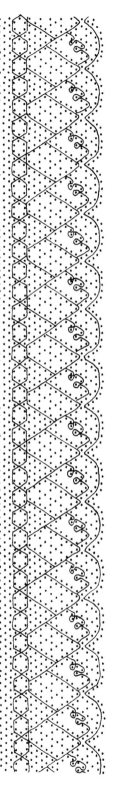

81

Pattern 17:
Slanting leaf II

Wind 29 pairs with 140, two pairs and one bobbin with 35/3. For the corner you need four extra pairs, wound with 140

The footing has two pairs of passives worked with cloth stitch. The rings along the footside and between the leaves are worked with honeycomb stitch. The gimp is passed

through a stitch at the points marked o. Work a cloth stitch (or a honeycomb stitch in the ring), pass the gimp through the pairs, put in the pin before or after the gimp, as shown on the diagram, and cover the pin. Work cloth stitch and two twists, pin and honeycomb stitch at the honeycomb pins in the scallop next to the leaf to make the

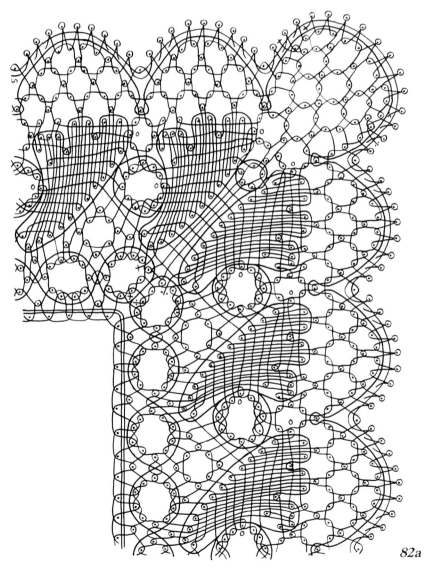

82a

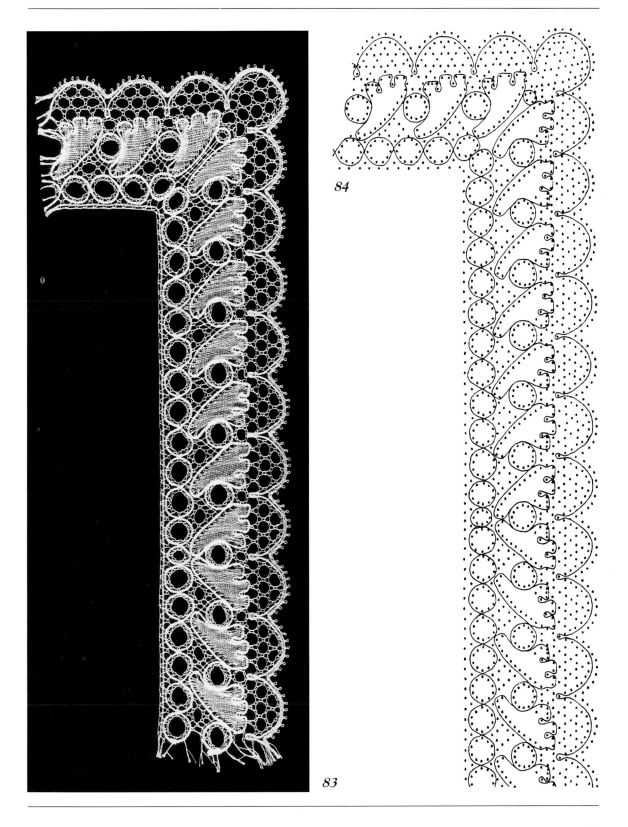

83

84

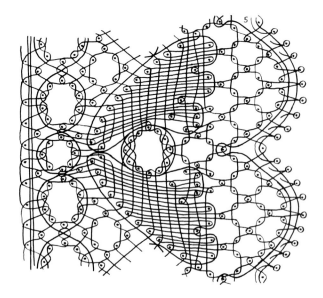

threads fit round the pins. The stitches without pins, along the middle ring and between the leaves in the corner, are cloth stitch and two twists.

In the corner you have to add four pairs, starting at +. When introducing a new pair in the ring in the bottom of the corner, hang the pair on the nearest pin, work some stitches, take out the pin, pull very carefully on one of the new threads, and replace the pin. When the corner is finished and the pairs have to be discarded at ÷, the easiest and most satisfactory method is to carry them with the gimp, i.e. let them follow the gimp for a short way as if they were part of it and then cut them off. *Note*: outside the pointed ends of the two leaves in the corner the threads are worked with a cloth stitch and twists without pin, instead of the usual honeycomb stitch. When you have finished the cloth-stitch filling in the first leaf of the corner, take the middle passive pair (out of the last three passives) and carry it with the gimp to the left through two pairs. Cross the gimps, let the pair pass round the other

gimp, and work honeycomb in the little ring. When the ring is finished, pass the pair round one gimp, cross the gimps, carry the pair with the other gimp through two pairs, and it will be in the corresponding place in the second leaf.

In the scallop, the pair used for the fourth and following picots is introduced shortly after the nook pin. Hang it on a pin and lay down the threads on each side of one of the passive threads, work until the fourth picot, take out the pin, carefully pull the new pair, and replace the pin. When discarding the pair, it is worked with cloth stitch among the other passive pairs, and after working two or three picots you can take away two threads. The introduced pair, the pair that works the picots, and the discarded pair are not necessarily the same pairs. At the same time, you have to introduce another pair. Hang it round the gimp outside the first stitch it works. When it is discarded, carry it with the gimp until after the nook pin.

The middle part should not pose any problems.

Pattern 18:
Great grandmother's locket

Wind 28 pairs with 140, three pairs with 35/3

The footing has two passive pairs, worked with cloth stitch; the catch pin is put in to the left of the ground stitch. Most of the lace is worked with honeycomb stitch. Be very careful with the gimp, especially round the two leaves between the lockets. Work the

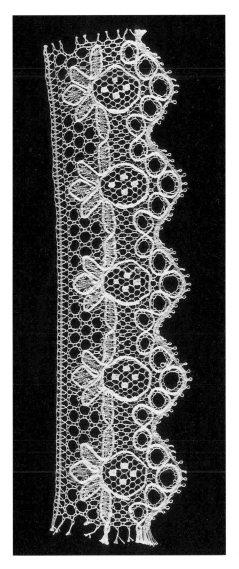

85

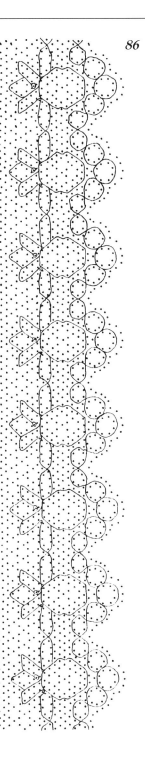

86

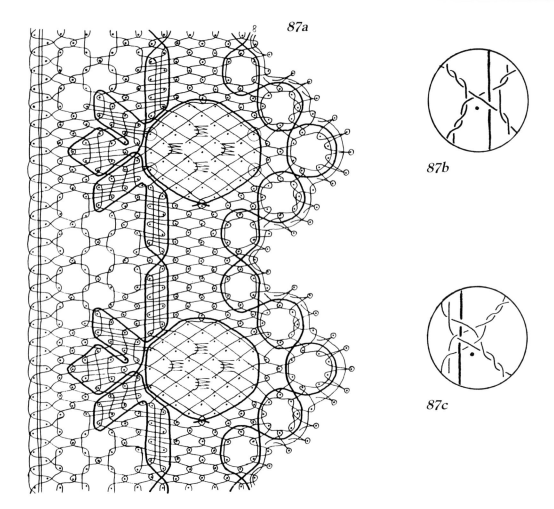

87a

87b

87c

pins outside the vertical gimps with cloth stitch and two twists, pin, honeycomb stitch, and pull the gimps quite hard. The gimp round the locket is a little tricky; the locket is supposed to be oval, but it has a tendency to be angular, so you have to cheat a little to improve its shape! At the top and bottom the gimp is passed through a stitch as described in 'Slanting leaf II'. Give the threads two twists outside and one inside the gimp. In the 'corners' (circled) to the right and to the left the gimps are passed through the stitches too, but this time on a slant. For the right-hand side, refer to diag. 87b. You will have two pairs with the gimp in the middle. Pass

the gimp over one thread to the right. Begin the half stitch, crossing the second thread over the third thread *and* the gimp. After this movement you will once more have two pairs with the gimp in the middle. Finish the stitch with three twists on the left pair and two twists on the right pair. The pin is inside the gimp.

For the left-hand side, refer to diag. 87c. You will have two pairs with the gimp in the middle. Pass the gimp over one thread to the right. Begin the cloth stitch, crossing the second thread over the third thread *and* the gimp, twist both pairs once. Again, pass the gimp over one thread to the right, cross the second thread over the third thread *and* the gimp. Once more you have two pairs with the gimp in the middle. Finish the stitch with one twist on the left pair and three twists on the right pair. The pin is inside the gimp.

This is how I work the locket, but there may well be a better method. *Note:* in the second step of the scallop the inner passive pair is passed round the gimp to work honeycomb stitch with the pair coming from the picot (*see* Pattern 15).

Pattern 19:
Bodil

Wind 31 pairs with 140, one pair: one bobbin with one thread and one with three threads 140, three pairs with 35/3

The odd pair is used as a passive pair in the footing, with three threads at the outer side. The pins between the passive pair and the blocks are worked with cloth stitch and two twists. Apart from the cloth stitch diamond, the whole pattern is worked with honeycomb stitches and no new features are added. *Note:* the number of holes in the repeat of the main pattern is uneven while the number of holes in the row of blocks is even so the actual repeat is two scallops long.

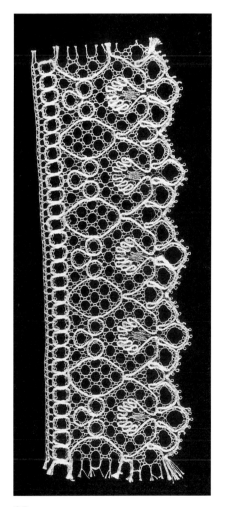

88

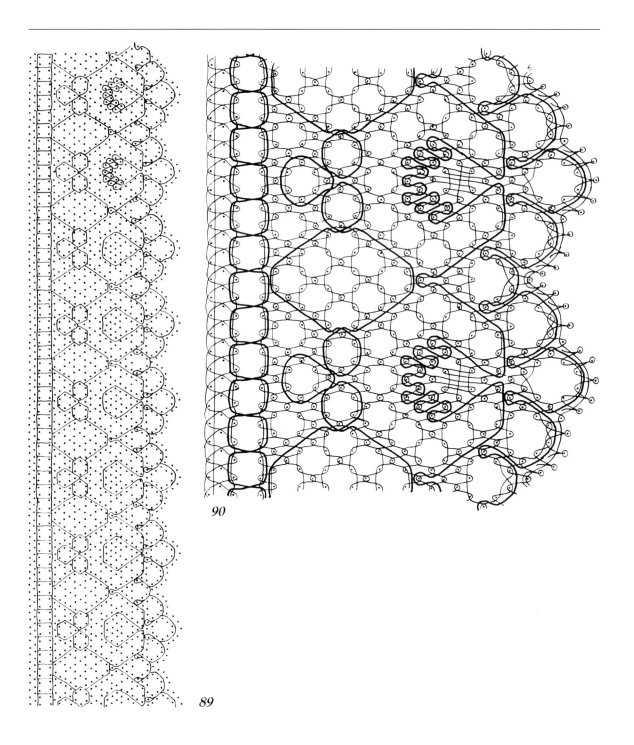

89

90

Pattern 20:
Lace with different figures

Wind 38 pairs with 140, two pairs with 35/2,
four pairs with 35/3

The two pairs with a thin gimp are used as
passive pairs in the footing, and in the head
worked with cloth stitch as normal pairs.
The headside is very dense, so if you wish
you can use double thread for the passive
pair instead of gimp.

91

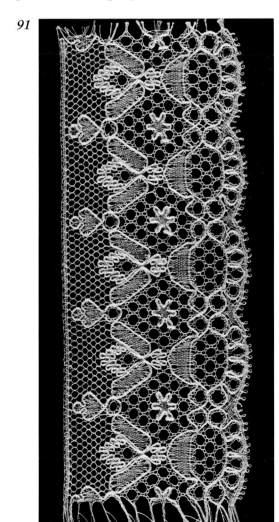

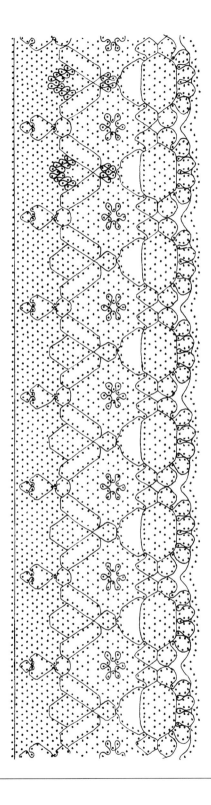

92

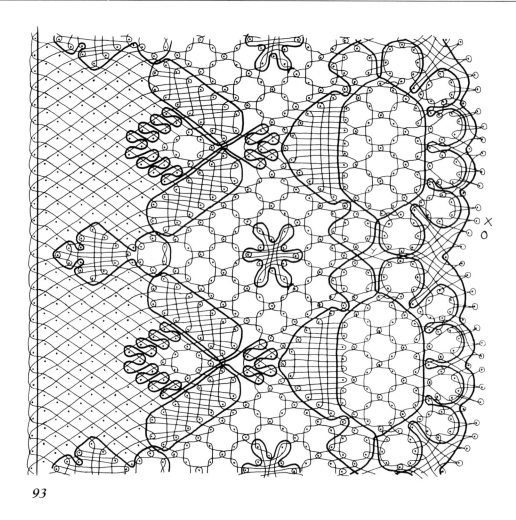

93

Most of the techniques for this pattern have already been described in previous patterns. Remember to work the pins in the honeycomb oval with cloth stitch and two twists, pin, honeycomb stitch, in the left-hand side, where one pair is coming from the cloth; it may be done in the right-hand side too. The starfish is worked in a new way, filled with cloth stitch which is an easier method than that used in the previous patterns.

The headside is the most difficult part of this pattern. In the nooks all the pairs are worked with cloth stitch, with one or two twists before and after the gimps. Work in the following order:

(i) Finish all the little rings of the scallop.

(ii) Work the last picot but two before the nook (x) and cloth stitch through the gimp pair and six pairs to the next ring.

(iii) Work the last picot but one (o) and cloth stitch through the gimp pair and five pairs to the ring. Work as much as possible inside this ring.

(iv) Work the last picot and cloth stitch through the gimp pair and five pairs to the ring.

(v) Work the nook pin and cloth stitch

through the gimp pair and five pairs to the ring.

(vi) Take the pair next to the passive gimp pair, cloth stitch through the gimp pair, work the picot and cloth stitch through the gimp pair and four pairs, twist three times, and work ground stitch at the bottom of the gimp nook.

(vii) Work the second picot with the next pair nearest the gimp pair and cloth stitch back through the gimp pair and one pair.

(viii) Work the third picot and cloth stitch through the gimp pair. All pairs are now ready for the next ring.

Work a cloth stitch and two twists without a pin in the space between the four rings inside the nook (y).

—7—
Three patterns in French Empire Style
and a singular design

Most Tønder patterns have a straight or slightly scalloped headside, but in the beginning of the nineteenth century some patterns were designed that were obviously influenced by the French Empire style. They have high, symmetrical scallops which are usually pointed, and a simplicity in the patterns which matches the style of buildings and furniture from this period.

Pattern 21:
French Empire I

Wind 20 pairs with 140, two pairs with 35/3

The passive pair in the footing is twisted after each stitch. Work honeycomb stitch in the little leaf and in the rings in the scallop. Where the gimps follow each other between the rings there are no twists between them. In the leaf there is a twist between the gimps.

Owing to the height of the scallop you need 12 passive pairs inside the nook pin, and the headside is worked in a different way from the usual method.

Begin in the nook. Pass the worker pair round all 12 pairs, which should be held together in a bunch as if they were one gimp thread. Twist the worker pair twice outside

the nook pin, and pass it round the 12 pairs as before, twist, pass it round the gimp thread and work honeycomb inside the gimp thread. You do not need to keep the passive pairs in order. Take the second pair from the outside, cloth stitch through the outer passive pair, work the picot, cloth stitch through one pair, and pass the worker pair round the bunch (ten pairs), twist, pass the worker pair round the gimp thread, and continue. The pair you choose as the outer passive pair will remain as the outer passive pair in the whole scallop. Continue in this way, taking a new worker pair from the bunch for every new picot, until only two passive pairs are left; they are worked with cloth stitch. *Note*: there is only one passive pair left at the very top. The work will be most pretty if you work the honeycomb stitch inside the gimp, to keep the pair from the picot in the right position before working the next picot.

When you reach the top, the easiest way to proceed is to work everything inside the scallop and all the rings before working the picots at the second side of the scallop. As soon as you have more than two passive pairs after the top, pass the worker pair round all the passive pairs but one, cloth stitch through one passive pair, work the picot, cloth stitch through one passive pair, and lay down the worker pair in the bunch

94

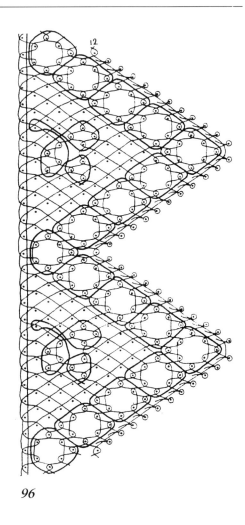

95

96

of passive pairs. Continue in this way until you reach the nook pin.

I can well understand why the lacemakers who made lace to earn their living worked in this way. It is much faster and it does not matter if the bobbins of the headside are not kept in order. The result is just as beautiful as if you have cloth stitched through all the pairs, sometimes even more so, because the latter method may look clumsy, with too many stitches squeezed together. The high scallops can be worked in a variety of ways, and two more are shown below.

Pattern 22:
French Empire II

Wind 33 pairs with 140, one pair with double 140, two pairs with 35/3

The double pair is used as a passive pair in the footing, and twisted after each stitch. It may seem a little odd that the flower in this somewhat stiff pattern is not symmetrical, but I like the way it is worked, and I think it improves the pattern to soften the design a little. The threads weave in and out between the gimps, where they follow each other. The two short pin chains in the oval honeycomb rings have a cloth stitch and two twists in the middle. No two rings in the scallop were identical in the old sample, but I preferred to work them all in the same way. If you happen to work some of the rings in another way, it does not matter, so long as the end result is pretty.

There are 12 passive pairs inside the nook pin plus one pair coming from the ring at the bottom. Begin in the nook. Use all the passive pairs in a bunch except the two outer pairs. Pass the worker pair round the bunch, cloth stitch through two passive pairs, twist the worker pair twice outside the nook pin, cloth stitch through two passive pairs, pass the worker pair round the bunch, twist, pass it round the gimp, and work honeycomb in the ring. Take the second pair from the right, cloth stitch through the outer passive pair, work the picot, cloth stitch through the outer passive pair and one pair from the bunch (take the one that is nearest at the time), pass the worker pair round the bunch, twist, pass it round the gimp, and work honeycomb in the ring. At the top you have only two passive pairs and here you work cloth stitch. After the top, the easiest method is to work everything inside the scallop and all the rings, before working the picots at the

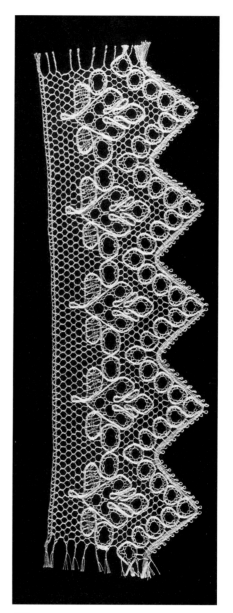

97

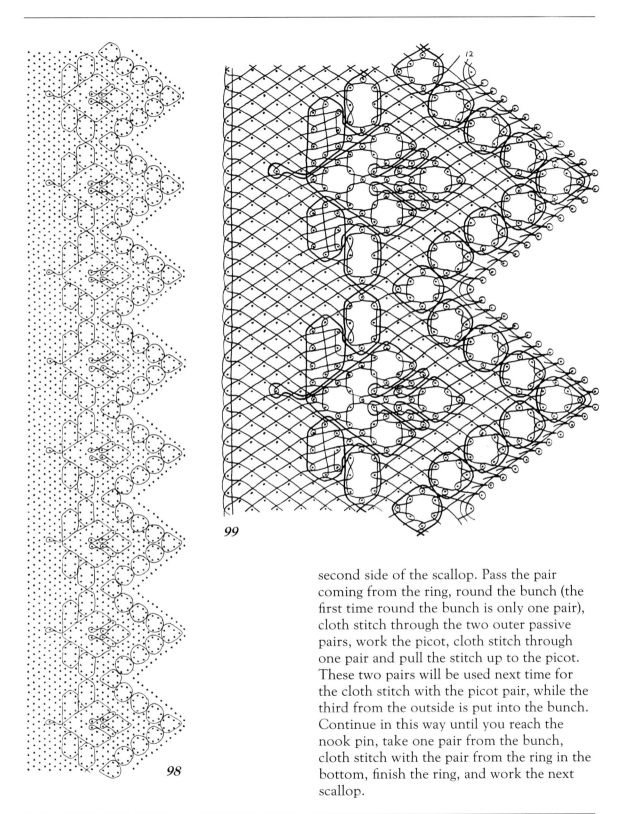

99

98

second side of the scallop. Pass the pair coming from the ring, round the bunch (the first time round the bunch is only one pair), cloth stitch through the two outer passive pairs, work the picot, cloth stitch through one pair and pull the stitch up to the picot. These two pairs will be used next time for the cloth stitch with the picot pair, while the third from the outside is put into the bunch. Continue in this way until you reach the nook pin, take one pair from the bunch, cloth stitch with the pair from the ring in the bottom, finish the ring, and work the next scallop.

Pattern 23:
French Empire III

Wind 31 pairs with 140, one pair: one bobbin with one thread and one with two threads 140, one pair with 35/2, two pairs and one bobbin with 35/3

The pair with the thin gimp is used as a passive pair in the footing, and worked with cloth stitch. The rose, sometimes called the tea-rose, is worked entirely in cloth stitch, and a cloth stitch and three twists is worked instead of a ground stitch outside the vertical gimps of the rose. Different ways to work the rose will be discussed in Patterns 31 and 32. The odd pair is used as the outer passive pair in the scallop, with the double thread at the outside. There are nine passive pairs inside the nook pin plus one pair coming from the honeycomb. As there are fewer passives than in the previous patterns, it is possible to work in the usual way.

Cloth stitch through all pairs, twist twice outside the nook pin, cloth stitch through all pairs, pass round the gimp, and work honeycomb. Take the second pair from the outside, cloth stitch with the outer passive pair, picot, cloth stitch through all passive pairs, pass round the gimp, and work honeycomb. There will be only two passive pairs at the top. Work in the opposite way at the second side of the scallop. If you prefer, you may use the passive pairs as a bunch and work cloth stitch through only one or two pairs.

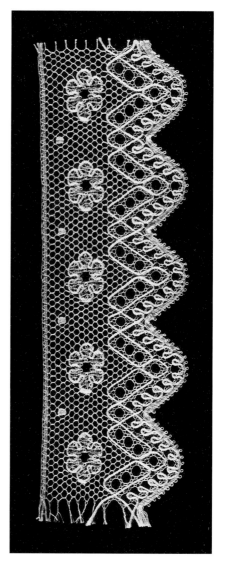

100

101

102

Pattern 24:
A singular design

For the lace: wind 12 pairs with 140, three pairs: one bobbin with 140 and one with 35/3, one pair with 35/3

For the insertion: wind ten pairs with 140, two pairs: one bobbin with 140 and one with 35/3, one pair with 35/3

103a

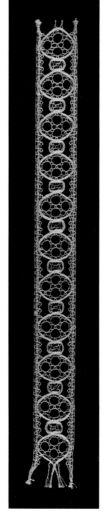

103b

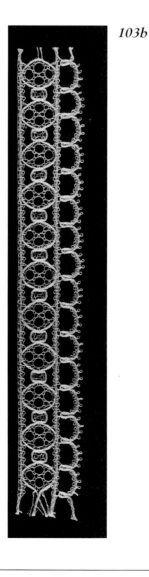

104

I found this lace (103*b*) among the old
samples, and the insertion (103*a*) came
naturally as a result of my work. The gimp
pair is used for the figure in the middle, the
odd pairs are used as passive pairs, either at
the footing, the centre straight line in the
lace, or the headside in the lace; all with the
gimp outside the thread. They are worked as
normal pairs with cloth stitch. The rest of
the pattern is worked with honeycomb stitch
except where indicated with a small *c* over
the stitch in the diagram: work cloth stitch
and two twists, pin, honeycomb stitch. *Note*:
the repeat is three scallops long. The
insertion is worked with a straight footing to
both sides, and the same pricking is used.

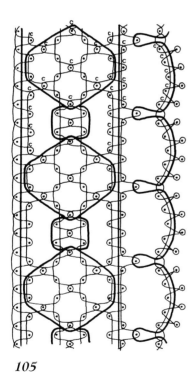

105

—8—

Floral patterns

Pattern 25:
Lace from a cuff

Wind 14 pairs with 140, one pair: one bobbin with one thread and one with two threads 140, one pair with 35/3

I found this lace on a little cuff, which was discovered in a sack full of old rags. I use it as a sort of introduction to the floral patterns where the threads are often worked in an irregular way, and where the size of the grid may change several times.

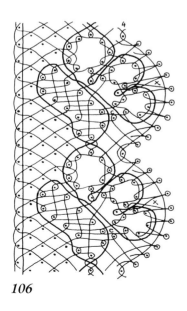

106

107

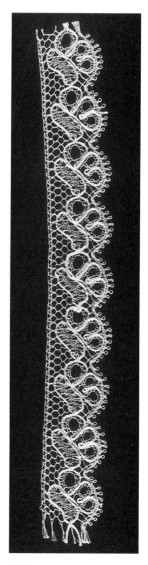

108

The odd pair is used as a passive pair in the footing, with the double thread at the outside. The *c* indicates cloth stitch and two twists, pin, honeycomb stitch. Work cloth stitch and twist with the pair coming from the last picot but two, where it passes through three pairs to enter the honeycomb ring. Work cloth stitch with the two pairs which cross inside the passive pairs in the head (*x*).

Pattern 26:
Lace with honeycomb scallop

Wind 21 pairs with 140, one bobbin with four threads 140, one pair and one bobbin with 35/3

One gimp is used as a passive in the footing. When the footing is worked like this, it is possible to use the passive to gather the lace if you want. It may be easier with a thinner gimp or with a double thread, if it is strong enough to stand the pull. The quadruple thread is used as a gimp outside the passive pairs in the headside. There is not much room for the gimps in the middle of the honeycomb, because it is made on a smaller scale than the rest of the lace. Use only one twist before and after the gimps, and make the threads change places between the gimps in the middle, in order to have them lying neatly together. *Note*: a ground stitch is used inside the gimp loops in the scallop.

When I first saw this pattern, I wondered if the peculiar way of using the outer gimp was a mistake, but as it is worked like this wherever I have found it, it must be the way it is meant to be worked. However, if you cannot bear to have an assymetrical scallop, you can work the gimp loops in the second half of the scallop too.

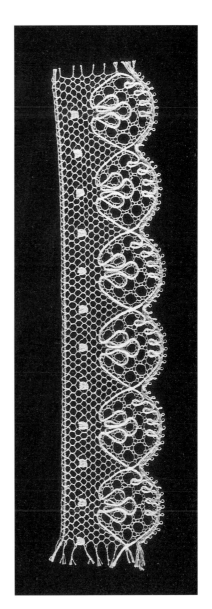

109

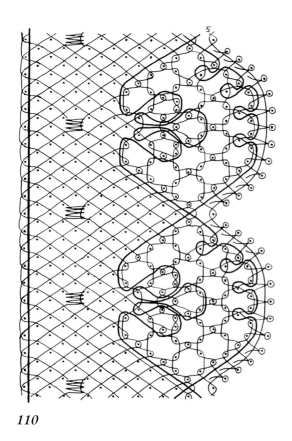

110

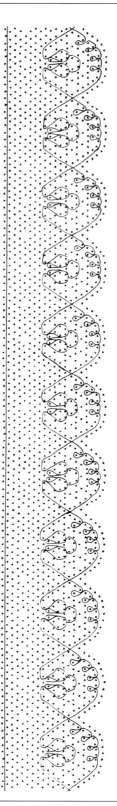

111

Pattern 27:
Lace with half-stitch scallop

Wind 19 pairs with 140, one pair: one bobbin with 140 and one with 35/2, two pairs with 35/3

The odd pair is used as a passive pair in the footing with the thin thread at the outer side. The honeycomb is worked with cloth stitch and two twists, pin, honeycomb stitch, as are the first four pins along the straight bottom of the half-stitch figure (x). The third pair from the right is used for each picot throughout the whole pattern. *Note*: the pairs change in the top of the scallop, and a gimp pair is introduced at the beginning of the flourish inside the half stitch and discarded at the end.

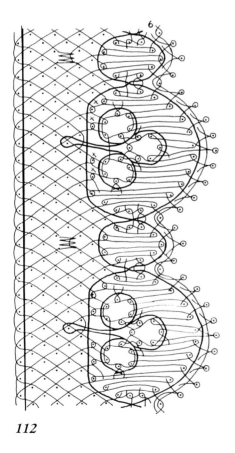

112

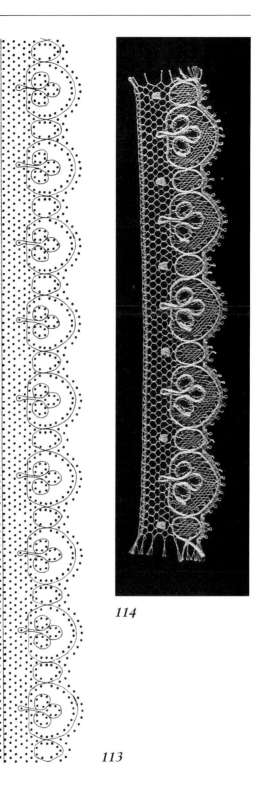

114

113

Pattern 28:
Insertion with big rings and tallies

Wind 14 pairs with 140, two pairs: one bobbin with 140 and one with 35/2, one pair with 35/3

The odd pairs are used as passive pairs in the footings with the thin thread at the outer side and worked with cloth stitch. In the big ring all pins are worked with cloth stitch and two twists, pin, honeycomb stitch. Do not work too far along the sides of the ring before you work the tallies; it makes your work easier if there is enough room for your movements. I used the tally with two twists round the outer passive threads, because it proved

116

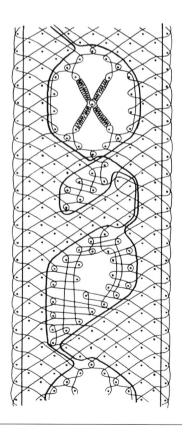

115

117

easier to keep the right shape in the long tallies. When starting a tally, work cloth stitch and two twists and put up the pin. Cover the pin by working the tally. After working the first two tallies, take the pair nearest the centre from each tally, twist twice, work cloth stitch and two twists, pin, cloth stitch and two twists. Twist the two outer pairs twice and work the next two tallies. Twist the pairs twice after the tallies, pin, and cover the pin with cloth stitch and two twists.

For some reason the lacemaker who made the old sample from which I made this reconstruction twisted the passive pair as well as the weaver pair round every pin in the cloth-stitch leaves, and therefore so did I; it gives a more open filling. If you prefer to work the usual way, do so. Where the gimps follow the same line between the leaves, the threads change places between them. *Note* the irregular way of working the ground in the nook between the small leaf and the stem, leading to the next leaf.

Pattern 29:
The snail

Wind 25 pairs with 140, two pairs with 35/3

The footing has one passive pair, worked with cloth stitch and twisted after each stitch. Work cloth stitch and two twists, pin, cloth stitch and the necessary number of twists at the pins marked z. In most of the pattern normal honeycomb is used, but work cloth stitch and two twists instead of honeycomb stitch where necessary. The short pin chains in the rings (x) are worked with a cloth stitch and two twists in the middle. A gimp pair is introduced at the top of the honeycomb filling. The gimp passes through three stitches in the concave side of the cloth figure. Work a cloth stitch, pass the gimp through both pairs, pin, twist the worker pair twice, cover the pin with cloth stitch, pass the worker pair round the gimp without twists, and continue with the filling. Twist the other pair twice before the honeycomb.

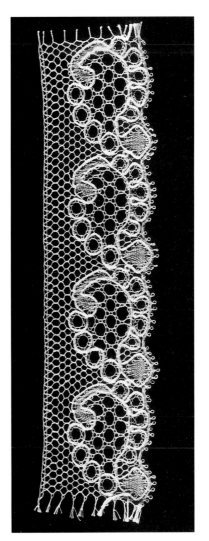

118

One pair lies as a sort of passive outside the gimp round the honeycomb filling; it is worked with cloth stitch. *Note*: at the top of the big scallop you find the exception that proves the rule: a picot in a nook (marked with an arrow on the diagram), not a very deep one, but a nook for all that.

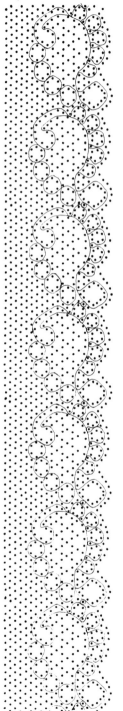

120

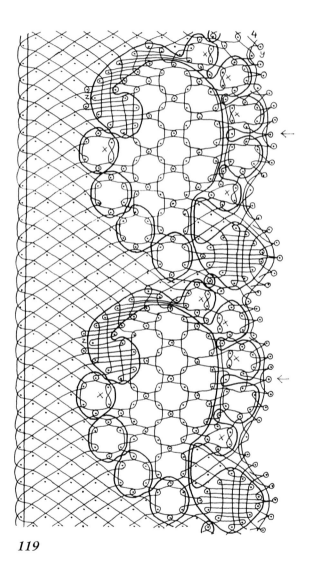

119

Pattern 30:
Daisy

Wind 29 pairs with 140, two or three pairs with 35/3

This pattern was worked in several different ways, and I have chosen two of them. In the first method the two parts of the pattern are separated, in the second a stem connects the

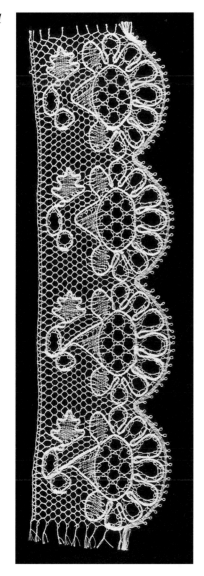

121

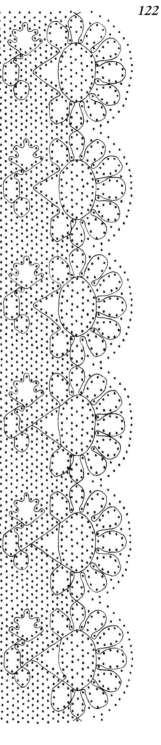

flower with the little flourish. For the latter you need only two pairs of gimp. The work is very similar, so choose the design you prefer. The footing has one pair, worked with cloth stitch. All the pins in the honeycomb are worked with cloth stitch and twists, pin, honeycomb stitch. If there are three stitches round a pin, only the first one is worked with cloth stitch. If you prefer the normal honeycomb, you have to remember

to cloth stitch at the six pins along the cloth triangle (x). The pins inside the first side of the triangle are also worked with cloth stitch and two twists, pin, honeycomb stitch, but they may be worked with just cloth stitch. There are two worker pairs at the nook pin which are crossed with cloth stitch and twist. The crossing pairs inside the nook pin are worked with cloth stitch and twist too.

123

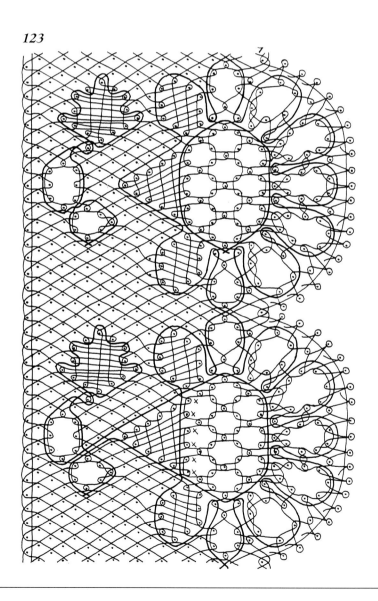

Pattern 31:
Insertion with roses

Wind 14 pairs with 140, one pair with 35/3

This pattern is not very complicated, but it gives you the opportunity of becoming familiar with the little rose before it appears in more intricate patterns. The footings are worked with one passive pair, twisted after each stitch. The open rose (diag. 124a) is worked with honeycomb stitch, except for in the side nooks where you have to work cloth stitch and two twists instead. You may give the pairs an extra twist, where they travel a long way from the honeycomb stitch through one pair with cloth-stitch and twist to the

124a

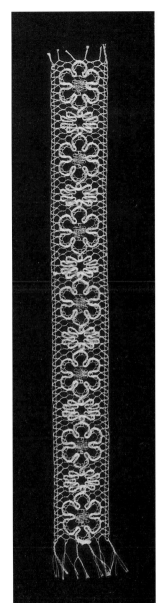

125a

cloth stitch diamond in the middle. Work in the opposite order after the diamond in the middle (x). *Note*: you have to work backwards for a little way in the nooks round the top and bottom petal.

The filled rose (124b) is worked entirely with cloth stitch. You may find many variations in the ways of working the middle of the rose: a honeycomb ring in the middle of the open rose, perhaps with a tally inside, a gimp round the middle etc. The two roses I have used in the samples are the most common. The pattern with the open rose is like the old lace, the pattern with the filled rose is worked to show another possibility. *Note:* the threads are worked in two different ways in the gimp loops.

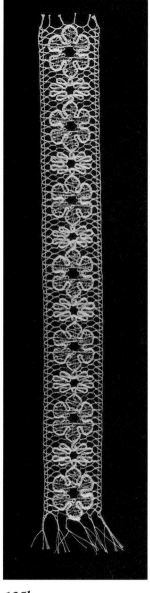

125b

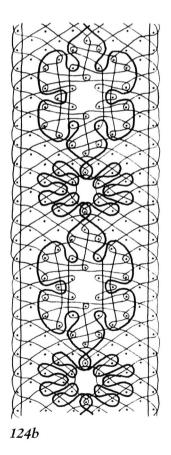

124b

126

Pattern 32:
Lace with roses and leaves

Wind 24 pairs with 140, one pair: one bobbin with one thread and one with two threads 140, two pairs with 35/3

The odd pair is used as a passive pair in the footing with the double thread at the outside. The roses are worked in a very similar manner to the open rose in the previous pattern; the only difference is that a ground stitch is used in the side nooks. For that reason you must work the sides of the rose before the second half of the cloth diamond, in order to get a nicely shaped gimp. Alternatively, you may choose to work cloth stitch in the nooks as is done in the roses in the previous pattern. In order to make the leaves beautifully curved the gimp must pass through a stitch twice in each leaf.

127

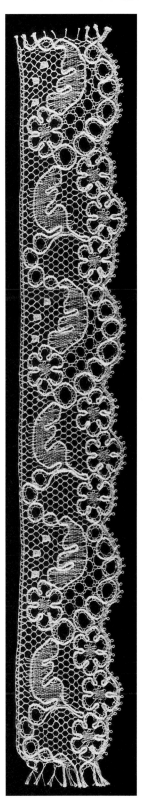

128

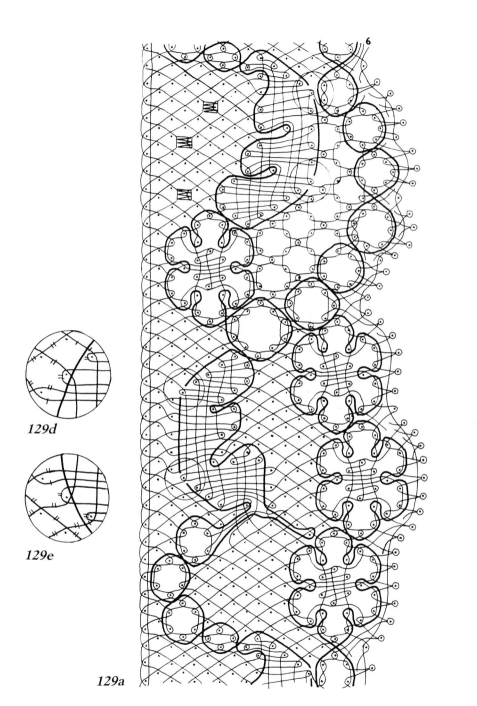

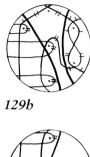

129b

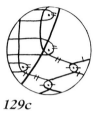

129c

129d

129e

129a

Look at diags 129a-e, where you can see how to work; the thin lines indicate pairs of thread, the thick line is a gimp. Diags 129b-c are for the leaf near the headside and diags 129d-e are for the leaf near the footside. *Note:* there are no twists round the gimp where it passes through a pair in the middle of the stitch. The number of picots does not match the number of stitches in the rings, so random picot pairs are taken out of the passive pairs to get the right number. Also, some pairs are taken from the passives into the rings to get enough pairs for the honeycomb stitches (*see* Pattern 15). This may well be worked in another way to achieve a similar result. The outer passive pair in the head is twisted after each stitch.

Big Rings

Before you work Pattern 33 it is necessary to explain how to manage when you have too many pairs inside a ring that is supposed to be big and open. I have drawn diag. 130a to show the way I draw a ring in a diagram, while diag. 130b shows in more detail how it is worked.

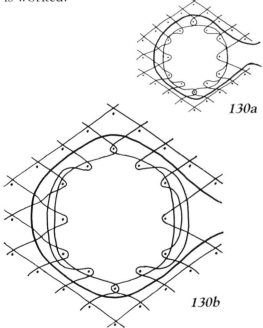

130a

130b

Work the top pin with honeycomb stitch, after the gimp has passed through all pairs. Look at the left-hand side first. All the pins are worked with honeycomb stitch. The pair that is going to lie as a passive pair between the honeycomb and the gimp is worked with cloth stitch. The pairs coming from the ground have no twists between the gimp and the passive pair, and one twist between the passive pair and the honeycomb stitch. Where the leaving pair meets an incoming pair, they cross with a cloth stitch. Another method is to carry the passive pair with the gimp and work as if it does not exist.

Now look at the right side. Again, all the pins are worked with honeycomb stitch. The passive pairs may be worked with cloth stitch as in the left-hand side, or they may be used as a gimp with the worker pair passing round both passive pairs before and after the honeycomb stitch. Sometimes you may prefer to combine the two methods, passing round the outer passive pair and working the other pair with cloth stitch.

Pattern 41 shows how the passives are used to replace the gimp, so that the ring appears round, even though the gimp may not fit closely around the pins (*see* right-hand side of diags 130a & b).

Pattern 43 shows how even a large number of spare pairs can be almost invisible if they are carried with the gimp, and also how they can be carried with the gimp round one ring to be used again in another.

Pattern 33:
Lace with grapes

Wind 30 pairs with 140, three pairs with 35/3

The passive pair in the footing has a twist after the stitch which brings the worker from outside into the ground. In this lace the ground is worked on different scales in different parts of the pattern, and it does not correspond to the scale of the honeycomb. *Note:* in some places a ground pair travels a different way than you would expect.

In the grapes there are one or two passive pairs in most of the rings; I have worked them with cloth stitch. *Note:* the number of pins in the sides of a ring between top and bottom pin is not necessarily the same. One gimp pair is introduced in the curve in the bottom of the big leaf (*x*), held in place by three ground stitches in a horizontal line. In the same way, ground stitch is used horizontally in the nook in the leaf to the left of the long stem (*y*). Two gimps are discarded, when they come to the little ring in the headside. They follow the gimp inside the ring through a few pairs and are then cut off.

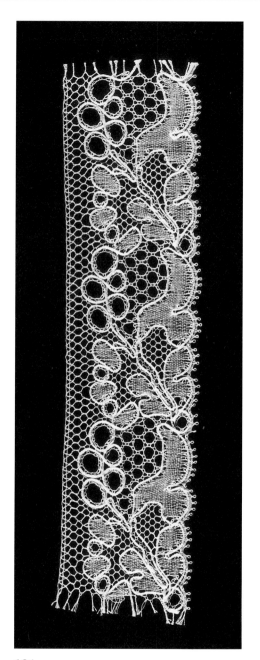

131

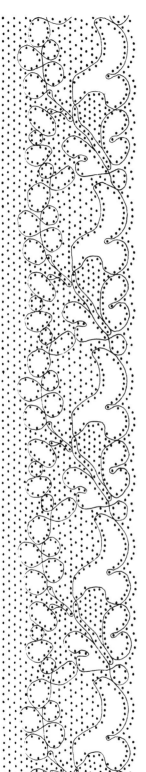

132

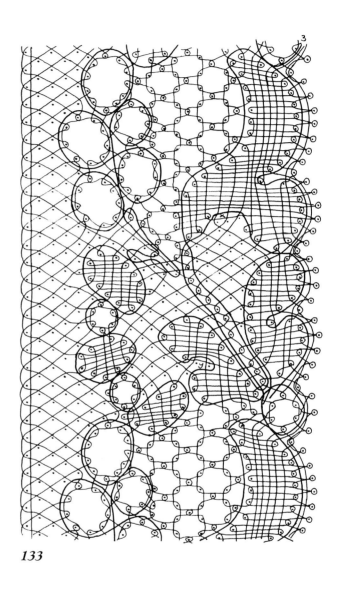

133

Pattern 34:
Koldinghus

Wind 28 pairs with 140, one pair: one bobbin with one thread and one with three threads 140, three pairs with 35/3

This pattern is named after an old castle in Kolding.

The odd pair is used as a passive pair in the footing with three threads at the outside. Two gimps pass vertically through the bottom of the big leaf; they are worked with cloth stitch like a normal pair while they are inside the cloth filling. The hip is worked entirely with cloth stitch, unless you prefer to cover the pins in the bottom loops with half stitch. A new gimp pair is introduced at the top of the rose and another in the middle. One gimp pair is discarded at the bottom of the hip and another at the bottom of the rose. In the ring in the middle of the rose all the pins are worked with cloth stitch and two twists, pin, honeycomb stitch.

The cloth may seem rather uneven, but this is in accordance with the old piece of lace, and I think it adds life to the pattern. The number of picots does not match the number of stitches in the rings, so various picot pairs are taken out of the passive pairs to get enough picots. Pairs are also taken from the passive pairs to enter the rings. The four repeats in my old piece of lace are worked in four different ways, so you do not have to be particular about how to work the headside. If the result is pretty, it is all right.

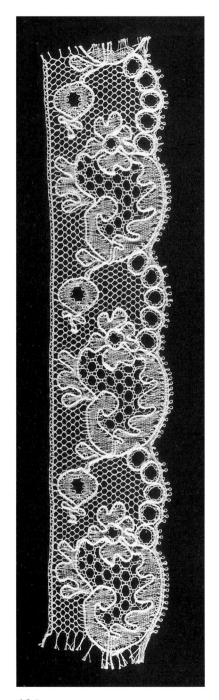

134

135

136

Pattern 35:
Lace with harebell

Wind 24 pairs with 140, one pair with double 140, three pairs with 35/3

The pair with double thread is used as a passive pair in the footing and it is worked with cloth stitch. Work ground stitch where the pin is put up to one side of a stitch outside a figure (x). Work cloth stitch and two or three twists where the pin is put up under a stitch (y). I have used ground stitch in the deep incisions in the big leaf; you may use cloth stitch, but the result will be a little stiffer. Work a cloth stitch before the pin in the honeycomb rings, whenever you find it necessary. Where two pairs cross without a pin inside the rings and between them, they are worked with cloth stitch and twists. Where two pairs cross in the ground without a pin, they are worked with ground stitch.

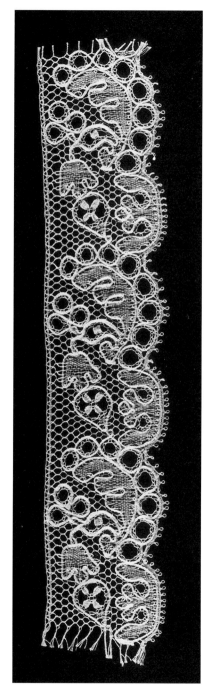

137

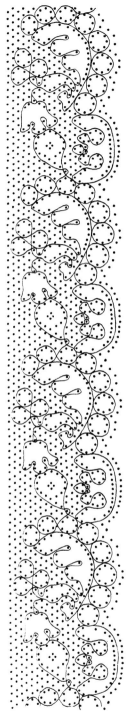

The most difficult feature in this pattern is the ring with the tallies and the tally in the small leaf. As in Pattern 28 I have used the tally shown in diag. 23*d*, with two twists round the passive threads. In this pattern there are four pins in the middle between the tallies, and they are worked with honeycomb stitch. *Note*: two gimps lie together in the same 'shed' above and below the small leaf, i.e. one from the left and one from the right, with no twists between them.

139

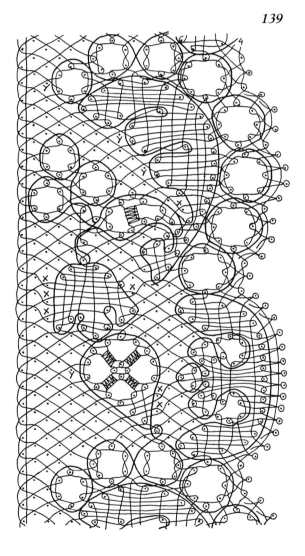

138

Pattern 36:
Lace from an old collar

Wind 36 pairs with 140, four pairs with 35/3

140

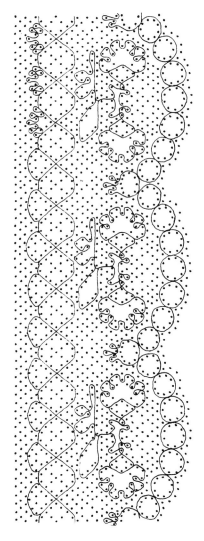

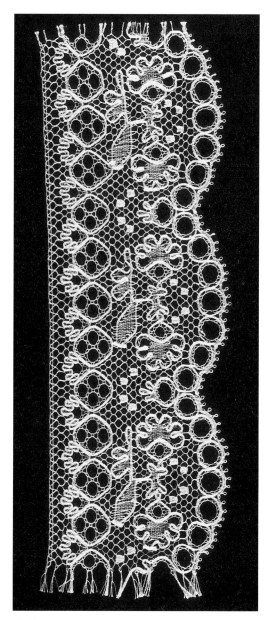

141

This lace is an odd mixture of a very regular and easy pattern along the footside and a rather irregular and more intricate pattern in the rest of the lace. It was not easy to reconstruct the old lace, because the gimp had nearly disappeared and all the repeats were full of holes, that should not have been there. But I hope that the result looks like the old lace as when it was new. The footing has one passive pair, worked with cloth stitch. The leaves and the unusual figure between the flowers are worked with cloth stitch. Remember to twist the pairs when they travel from the cloth stitch diamond in the middle of the flower to the honeycomb stitches along the gimp. There are no twists between the gimps where they lie together.

The oval ring inside the nook pin is a little special. All the pins on the left-hand side are worked with cloth stitch, together with the cloth stitch in the loops to the side of the ring. The right-hand side is worked with honeycomb stitch. A passive pair is carried with the gimp in the two neighbouring rings, and another passive pair lies outside the middle honeycomb stitch in the right-hand side of the oval ring. If the pairs were not worked like this, it would be impossible to work the gimps as they are.

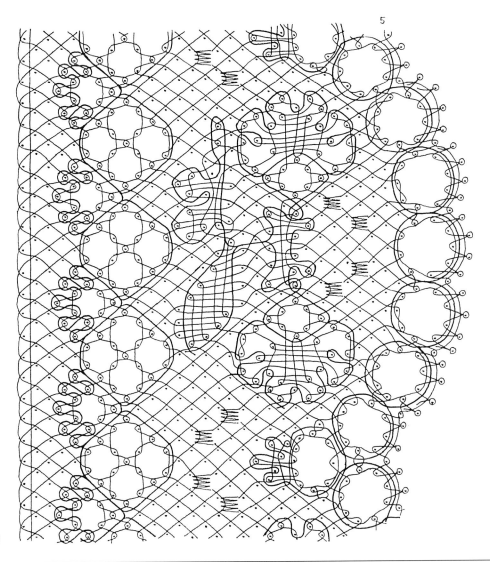

142

Pattern 37:
Lace with roses and hanging leaves

Wind 53 pairs with 140, two pairs: one bobbin with 140 and one with 35/2, five pairs with 35/3

My model for this pattern was rather worn and crumbled and the footing was missing, so it was difficult to know the right size and you may add more ground if you want. The old pattern was pricked on a smaller scale than mine. It is a great help if you are familiar with the 'little rose', before you work this pattern (*see* Pattern 31). The odd pairs are used as a passive pair in the footing and as the outer passive pair in the head, both with the gimp at the outside. The three large hanging leaves are worked in the same way except for the veins in the middles. In the first leaf you work ground stitch from right to left; in the second leaf you twist the passive pairs between the gimps and in the third leaf you work ground stitch from left to right. There is no pin to support the worker pair from the vein where it becomes a passive pair in the cloth, so you have to pull this passive and the one to its left to the right-hand side when working the cloth. *Note*: a gimp pair is introduced to surround the first and second large leaf, while the third leaf is surrounded by the gimp from the stem.

It is difficult to judge how many twists you need to use between the gimps lying together. The number must be adjusted to the amount of space, from no twists at all to a maximum of three, in some places between the roses. Work cloth stitch and two twists, where two pairs are crossing without pins to both sides of the nook. Also work cloth stitch and twists between the gimps in the beginning of the curved line inside the roses. Work cloth

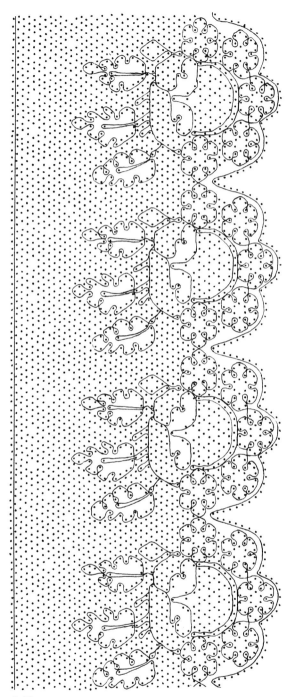

143

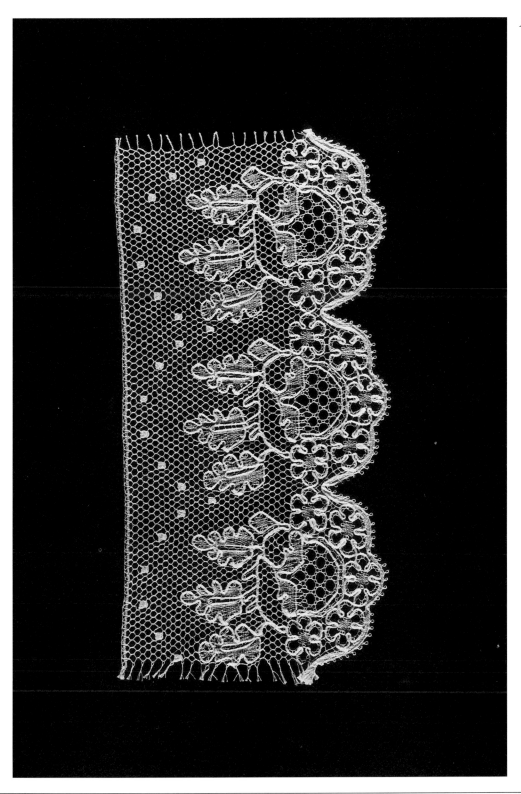

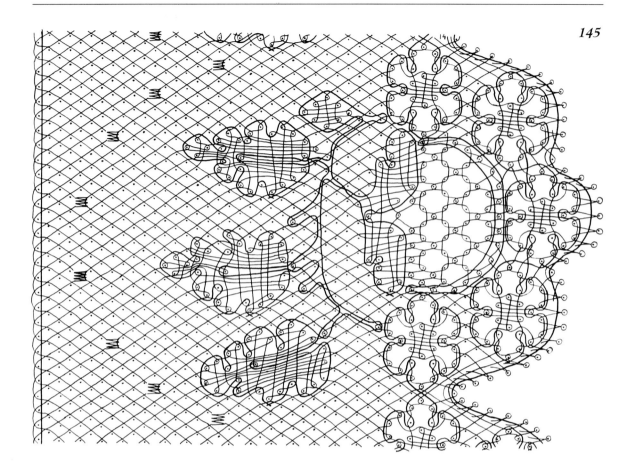

stitch and twists in the ground and in the honeycomb every time you find it necessary.

There are 14 passive pairs at the nook pin. Pass the worker pair round 12 pairs and cloth stitch through two pairs (the outer pair is the one with the gimp), twist the worker pair twice, cloth stitch through two pairs, pass round 12 pairs, and twist twice before going on in the pattern. Take the second pair from the outside, cloth stitch through the outer pair, picot, cloth stitch through two pairs, pass round the rest, twist twice, and go on in the pattern. Go on like this until only five passive pairs are left, by which time you should be at the 'corner' of the second rose. From now on work cloth stitch through all

the passive pairs. You still take the second pair from outside for the picot, and work the headside in the usual way, until you have more than five passives at the 'corner' of the fourth rose. Pass the worker pair round all the pairs but two, cloth stitch through two pairs, picot, cloth stitch through the outer pair and leave the worker pair as the second pair from outside. Go on in this way until you reach the nook pin.

It is a little difficult to work the picots underneath the scallop, but it might help a little if you take the outer gimp, pull it to the left round all the pins, and leave it at the back of the pillow. Like this it will hold the other passives in check until you have finished the picot.

Pattern 38:
Stinne Winther

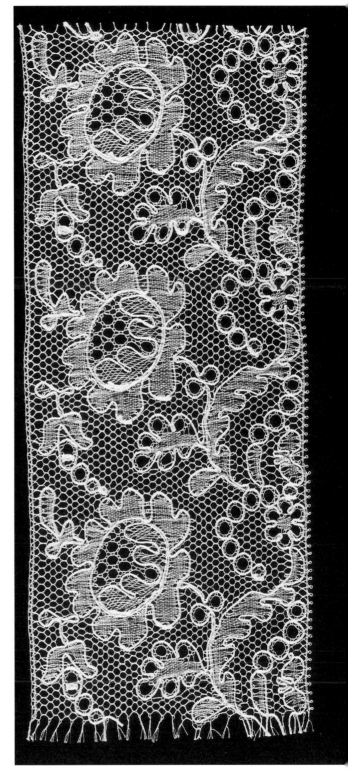

Wind 53 pairs with 140, one pair with double 140, six pairs with 35/3

The pair with double thread is used as a passive pair in the footing, worked with cloth stitch and twisted every second time. In this pattern you will in some places see the pin outside the vertical gimp worked with cloth stitch and three twists (x), and in other places with a ground stitch to the side of the pin (y). It has to do with the shape you want; the first way pushes the gimp towards the figure it surrounds while the second allows the gimp to straighten. Where the figure is a little concave, the cloth stitch way is the best, and if the figure is convex, use the ground stitch way. Nevertheless, I have worked cloth stitch and three twists to the side of all honeycomb rings, but this is not a dictate; use the other method if you prefer. Work the two pins at z with cloth stitch and three twists and put up the pins to the right-hand side of the stitch.

In some places the gimp is passed through a stitch and the way to work thus is shown in Pattern 32. Only one gimp travels through the whole lace, all others are introduced and discarded continuously. One gimp pair is introduced at the top of the little flourish next to the footing (A) and discarded in the bottom. Two gimp pairs are introduced in the top of the big flower, one in the middle and one round the petal to the right (B and C). They are discarded at the bottom, one in the middle and one in the bottom of the petal on the right. *Note*: two gimps cross at the bases of the right-hand vertical nooks in the big flower. In the big flower you see the half stitch as a contrast to the surrounding cloth stitch. A new gimp pair is introduced, where the half-stitch filling begins (D), so there are two gimps between the half stitch and the cloth stitch all the way. The introduced gimp pair is discarded when the half-stitch filling is finished. One gimp pair is introduced for the little stem with the harebell (E). You may begin at the end closest to the big flower or at the top of the diamond, as you find most convenient. The gimp is discarded at the end of the figure. One gimp pair is introduced for the stem coming from the big flower (F). Near the

headside, two gimp pairs are introduced, one at the beginning of the short string of rings (G), and one at the beginning of the tiny figure (H); the latter is discarded in the end of the figure. One gimp pair is discarded in the end of the long string of rings, and one is discarded along the big leaf, as I will explain further. Where the big leaf and the stem from the big flower meet, there is a ground stitch without a pin to the left of the stem,

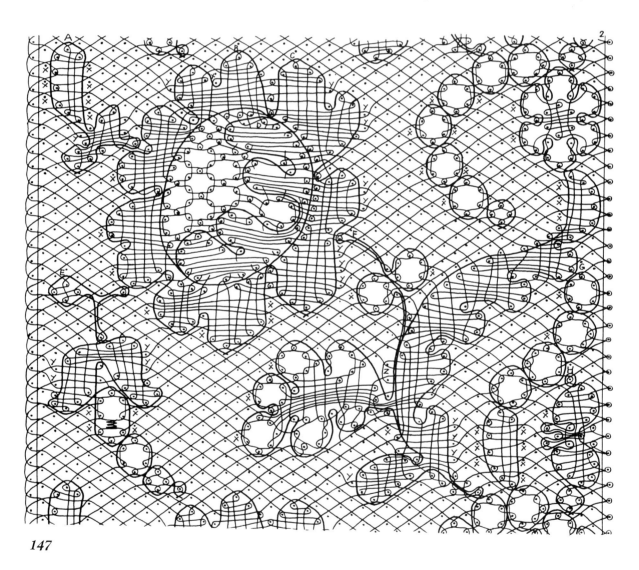

147

and there you will have three gimps together. Use the two right-hand gimps as one and keep them together until you are beyond the small leaf with holes. Now you will have three gimps together again. Discard the gimp in the middle, after the worker pair from the big leaf has passed round the gimps two or three times. The remaining two gimps stay together until the nook, where the very small leaf begins. Discard the left-hand one. I have used only six gimp pairs, though it looks as if there are more; the same gimp pairs are used in different figures in the same repeat. If you work in a different order, you may need seven gimp pairs. The headside is worked with two passive pairs, the outer twisted after each stitch. Work cloth stitch and twists inside the passive pairs. If you want, you may work this pattern as an insertion.

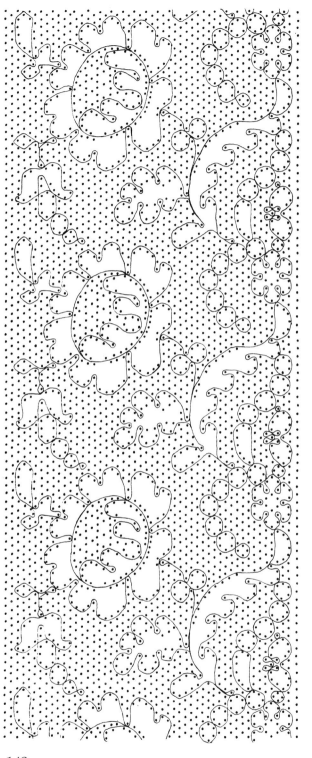

148

Pattern 39:
Lace without ground

Wind 22 pairs with 140, two pairs with 35/3

This pattern was found in a late eighteenth-century sample book and it is one of the very few patterns with a curved footside.

The footing is very simple. Pass the footside pair from inside, round the gimp, twist twice outside the pin, pass the footside pair round the gimp again and twist. The leaves are worked with cloth stitch, and the small circles and ovals with half stitch. In the big leaf a new pair is introduced ($+1$). The worker pair comes from the right-hand side. Work cloth stitch with the worker and the footside pair, put up the pin and hang the new pair round it, cover the pin by working cloth stitch through the new pair and the rest of the passives. Keep the same worker pair, the new pair becomes the footside pair, and the old footside pair becomes a passive pair in the cloth stitch (151a). When the worker pair comes back to the footside, take away the pin, pull the new pair slightly, and replace the pin, now holding only the two old pairs. At the start of the pricking, this pair is already present in the lace. One pair is discarded level with ($\div 1$). As the cloth stitch is very dense in the left-hand side, it helps to take out two threads here, not necessarily the new ones but perhaps two threads that are coming to an end. The gimps cross in the same 'shed' between the circles, apart from the few places where there is enough room for the threads to change places.

The almost circular curve after the small circles is a little complicated. Work cloth stitch all over as far as possible; then the worker pair goes to and fro through only a few passive pairs, before it returns to the other side of the cloth (you can see the same

149

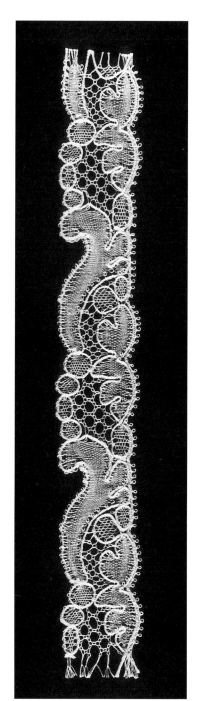

150

method used in the butterfly shaped leaf in the headside). Take the footside pair after the last pin inside the gimp (x), pass it round the gimp, twist twice outside the pin, pass it round the gimp, and carry the pair with the gimp. Take the left-hand passive pair, pass it round the gimp and the former footside pair, twist twice outside the pin, pass it round the gimp and pair, and carry one more pair with the gimp. Take the next passive pair, pass it round the gimp and two pairs, twist twice outside the pin, pass it round the gimp and two pairs. Take the footside pair, pass it round the gimp, put up the pin in the nook, twist the pair twice outside the pin, and pass it round the gimp. You may leave out the twist on the footside pair inside the gimp at the first pins after the nook as there is not much room here. The two passive pairs carried with the gimp become passive pairs again along the footside.

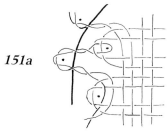

151a

Note: the little loop of the big leaf is worked on its own and only connected with the rest of the leaf in one place (y), where the worker travels through all passives. You must use at least two, preferably three twists after the gimp, where it follows the concave curve of the big leaf to press the gimp into the right position. The honeycomb is worked in the usual way except for the stitch (c) which is worked with cloth stitch and two twists. *Note*: just before the point where the big leaf comes to the headside you must discard a gimp pair. After the leaf it is re-introduced. This lace may be mounted either with the fabric following the footing in all its curves or by sewing only the spots that are on a straight line to a hem.

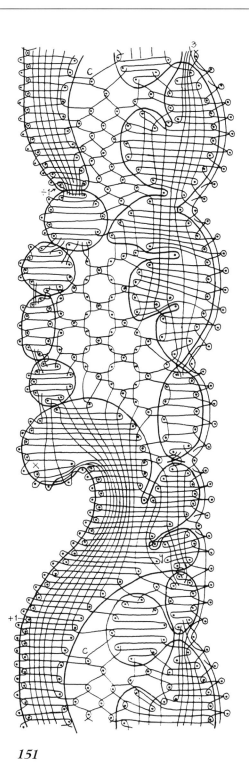

151

Pattern 40:
Rococo

*Wind 31 pairs with 140, one pair with 35/2,
two pairs with 35/3*

The thin gimp pair is used as a passive pair in
the footing, worked with cloth stitch. The
different scales of the grids result in a pattern
where the ground outside the figures is rather
open and loose, so you must be careful not
to take away the pins too soon.

In the elder blossom filling the pin chains are
worked with cloth stitch and three twists to
give a firm filling with very distinct holes.
The honeycomb filling is worked in an
unusual way: the top and bottom pins in the
small hexagons are worked with honeycomb
stitch as usual, but all the pins in between,
on the diagonal lines, are worked with cloth
stitch and three twists. This is the only lace
where I have seen this way of working
honeycomb and I was curious as to the
reason. The only explanation I can imagine is
that worked like this it matches the other
filling very well. In three places two gimps lie
together with only one row of pins between
(A,B,C). They are all worked with cloth
stitch and twist. Also work cloth stitch and
twist where two pairs cross without pins
between the gimps, to the left of the very fine
ground (below C). The gimps may easily lose
their shape here, so pull them very carefully.
Work cloth stitch and twist in the little ring
in the headside and in the four-pin bud in the
cloth. The scallop to the right of the elder
blossom filling is worked entirely with cloth
stitch, and the worker is twisted once before
it works cloth stitch with the picot pair. The
picot pair is twisted on both sides of the
gimp. *Note* the way the nooks are worked,
and that in some places a new worker is
taken from the passive pairs outside the

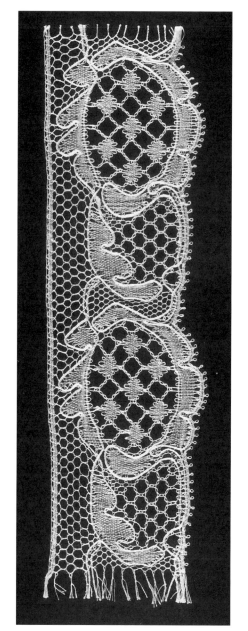

152

gimp: twist the passive pair next to the gimp,
pass it round the gimp, twist, and cloth stitch
through all the passive pairs, including the
former worker pair.

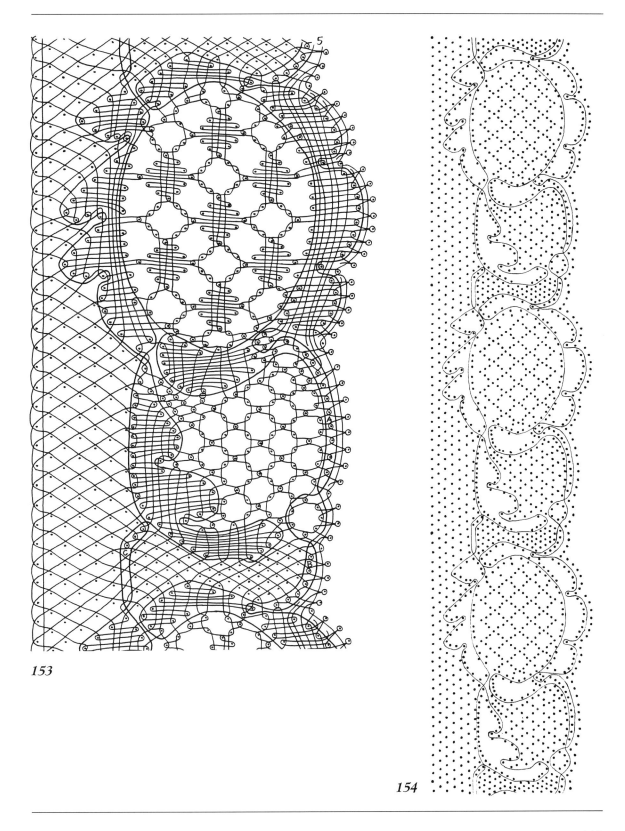

153

154

Pattern 41:
Insertion with a big flower

Wind 50 pairs with 140, four pairs with 35/2,
three pairs with 35/3

The four pairs with a thin gimp are used as
passive pairs along the footside, worked with
cloth stitch on each side of the open edging.
Work normal honeycomb in the middle of
the edging, and cloth stitch and two twists,

155

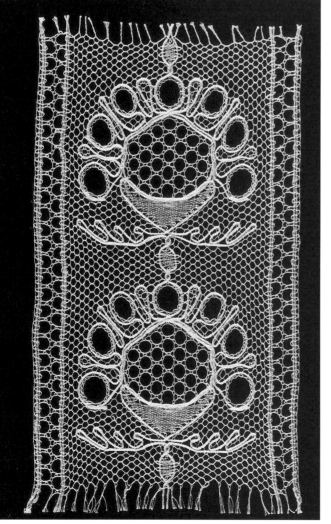

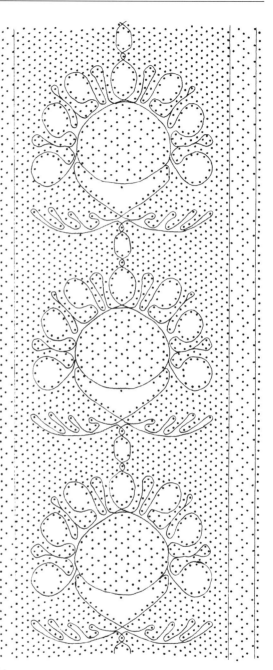

156

157

pin, honeycomb stitch to the two sides. The
ground pins just inside the passive pairs are
worked with ground stitch and the pins
outside both pairs. One gimp pair comes
from the top to the flower and surrounds the
first big ring (the way to work the big rings is
explained on p. 101). Introduce two new
gimp pairs round the two four-pin buds to
the sides. Work cloth stitch and three twists
between the new gimps and those in the
middle. Cross all four gimps beneath the top
ring; the threads may or may not change
places, depending on your preferred working
method (*see* diag. 157a). To the sides of the

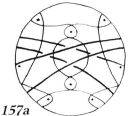

157a

honeycomb the gimps are separated by the
threads, at the base they are kept together.
You may separate them all the way round or
keep them together, as you prefer. The rings
are worked in different ways, but all of them

use the working method explained under 'Big rings'.

There are no twists between the gimps in the small twigs that jut out between the rings. *Note* the irregular ground above the last ring in each side (x); one pair travels across the regular ground and the gimps with two stitches without pins. Discard one gimp pair in each side at the bottom of the last rings. In the sepals beneath the flower you must keep all the twists in the ground between the small twigs in order to push the gimps together; there are no twists between the gimps in each twig.

In most of this pattern the ground is pricked in curved lines. You cannot use a regular grid, because the scale changes almost invisibly, especially round the sepals. That is why the ground is worked in an unusual way at the end of most of the small twigs.

Pattern 42:
Lace with a leaf of rings and circles

Wind 24 pairs with 140, one pair with 35/2, two pairs and one bobbin with 35/3

In a small group of patterns the greater part of the design is made up mainly of big rings, sometimes filled, but very often open, using the technique of pairs carried with the gimp. This pattern and the next are rather different examples of this particular working method.

One bobbin with a thick gimp is used as the passive in the footing. The pair with a thin gimp is used as a passive pair in the head, together with a normal pair outside the gimp pair. There are six passive pairs inside the gimp pair at the nook pin, i.e. a total of eight passive pairs.

At the nook pin: pass the worker pair round six passives, cloth stitch through the gimp pair, twist, cloth stitch and twist with the outer pair, pin, cloth stitch and twist with the outer pair, cloth stitch through the gimp pair, and pass round six passives. Inside the passive pairs you have one or two twists, depending on the distance between the passive pairs and the first pin inside. Take the pair next to the gimp pair for the picot,

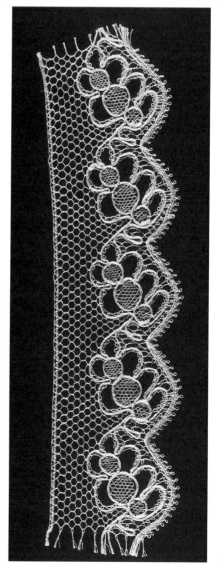

158

cloth stitch through the gimp pair, twist,
cloth stitch and twist with the outer pair,
picot, cloth stitch and twist with the outer
pair, cloth stitch through the gimp pair, pass
round the rest of the passive pairs and twist.
When all the passive pairs inside the gimp
pair have come to an end, the headside
worker pair is travelling out and in, as seen
in the diagram. The honeycomb is worked
with cloth stitch and two twists, pin,
honeycomb stitch everywhere; this is the best
way to work when the threads are travelling
as irregularly as here. When the pointed ring
at the top is finished, you can work the right-
hand side of the leaf almost to the end. A
new gimp pair is introduced, where the half-
stitch circles begin. Work the first circle and
the first ring to the left, and after that the two
other circles and the last section of the
bottom ring on the right. Discard the gimp
pair from the half-stitch circles, when the last
circle is finished. Now it is easy to work the
last ring to the left and the small gap before
the next repeat.

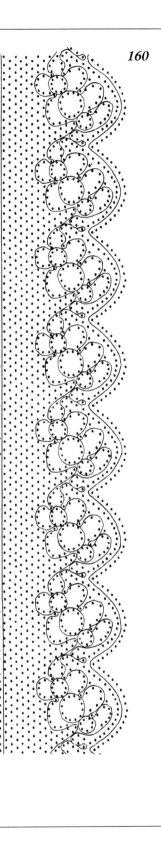

160

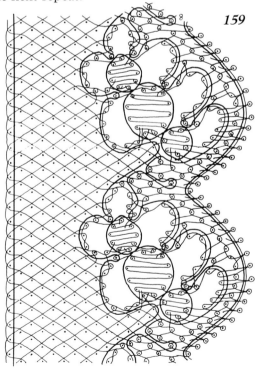

159

Pattern 43:
Lace with a high scallop of rings

Wind 46 pairs with 140, two pairs with double 140, four pairs 35/3

The technique of carrying pairs with the gimp is used to its utmost in this pattern. It is not an easy pattern, but fascinating to work, and if you have come to understand the system, you can work it relatively quickly.

One double pair is used as a passive pair in the footing, worked with cloth stitch. The other one is used as the outer passive pair in the headside, worked with cloth stitch and twist. Throughout this pattern the honeycomb is worked with cloth stitch and two twists, pin, honeycomb stitch. Many pins in the scallop are worked with pairs coming from unexpected directions and taken out of the passive pairs; this way of working the honeycomb gives the best result.

See diags 162a-b. The small figure in the ground is not complicated. Two pairs of gimp threads are introduced for the figure. Work cloth stitch inside the stem, and carry one pair with the gimp from the little twig near the top and round the corner to take part in the ground again (x). Work cloth stitch and two twists in the ground, where indicated with (c). The interior of the rings has honeycomb inside the gimp, and the middle has been worked in two ways; for the first see diag. 162a and the two top repeats on photo. 161. Work cloth stitch and two twists without pin to the sides of the tally. It may be difficult to get a pretty tally, as it is only held in its place by a pin between the two threads of each pair. It helps to use the tally with two twists round the passives in the sides.

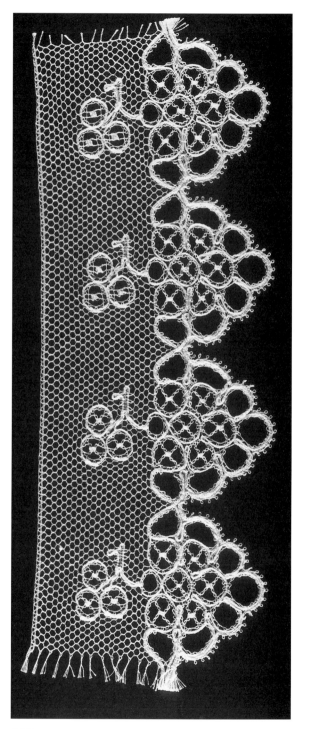

161

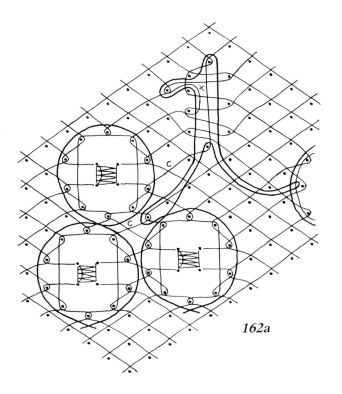

162a

The second way may be a little easier (*see* diag. 162*b* and the two lower repeats on photo. 161). Work the four central pins with cloth stitch and two twists, and the tally in the middle with the two inner pairs; the outer pairs are lying to the sides of the tally. The gimp that forms the twig and touches the central bottom ring in the scallop crosses another gimp and the left-hand pair in the honeycomb stitch, but it does not travel round the pin. For that reason you have to finish the honeycomb ring in the scallop before you pass the gimp from the little figure back to the stem. Only in this way will you get the right shape of ring and stem.

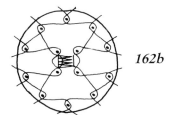

162b

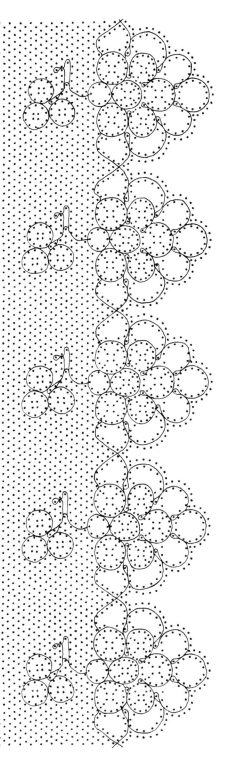

163

162c

Now see diag. 162c. There are 18 pairs inside the nook pin, the outer one is the one with the double thread. Two gimp pairs cross inside the nook pin, and two gimps follow each other round the beginning of the ring. Pass the worker pair round 17 pairs, cloth stitch and twist with the double pair, give the worker an extra twist, pin, cloth stitch and twist with the double pair, pass round 17 pairs, and pass round the two gimps.

Working the picots, take the third pair from outside, cloth stitch with one pair, twist, cloth stitch and twist with the double pair, picot, cloth stitch and twist with the double pair, cloth stitch with one pair, pass round the passive pairs, and pass round the gimp. Work like this as long as you have more than three passive pairs. Work cloth stitch throughout, when there are two or three passive pairs, left, i.e. round the three top rings.

In this pattern the best way to work is to carry all passive pairs in the rings with the gimp. There is not much room and there are many passives, so it would be too clumsy to work with cloth stitch through the passives. Start at the left-hand side of the first ring. You will have three passives carried with the gimp. Keep them in their order and take them again, one by one, to the bottom of the ring. Go on working the right-hand side. After the first two picots you have to take two pairs out of the passive pairs outside the gimp pair and carry them with the gimp pair around the ring. The easiest way is to pass them round the gimp pair and let them stay inside the gimp pair like the passive pairs on the other side, until you need them in the pattern. When you come to the first nook pin in the headside (y), the worker pair being outside the pin, cloth stitch through two pairs, and pass the worker pair round the bunch of passive pairs as usual, cloth stitch through three pairs coming from the ring, pin (in the gimp nook (z)), and cover the pin. Pass the gimp back through four pairs and then through four more pairs taken out of the passive pairs to work honeycomb stitch inside the next ring. There are now ten pairs outside the gimp, and after the next picot you will have nine passive pairs round the ring until the next nook.

Note: outside the next ring you have to change the worker pair twice to get two extra

picots. In the next nook, take four passive pairs and carry them with the gimp to the inside of the ring, and take one pair to the next ring. There are now four pairs outside the gimp, and after the next picot you will have three passive pairs round the ring until the next nook. Again you have to change the worker pair to get extra picots. In the next nook, take one passive pair to the inside of the ring, and you will have two passive pairs left to travel round the top. After the top the other side of the scallop is worked in the opposite way.

The rings in the middle of the scallop are worked with a tally in the middle, hanging in short pin chains, worked with cloth stitch and two twists. The first filled ring is worked with one passive pair to the right (w) in such a way as to permit the gimp to go round a pin and back along itself. The ring on the right side of the gimp loop is worked in a similar way. Very often in this lace you have to work nearly backwards. Do not go too far in the outer part of the scallop even if you are able to, since it will complicate the work. You have to work the outer rings in the second half of the scallop before you pass the gimps into the deep nooks. Here you must be very careful when you put the pin into the hole as it is not easy to see which is the right one.

It may be difficult to work the picots in the last part of the scallop. Take the outer (double) pair, pull it to the left and round the pins, and leave it at the back of the pillow to hold the other passive pairs in their places, while you work the picot. As the picot pins usually slant slightly outwards, you will have very little room when you work the picots at the beginning of a scallop. Push down the pins in the last part of the previous scallop, so only the pin for the new picot is raised over the surroundings. When the picot is finished, push down the pin in order to give room for the next picot.

−9−
Later patterns

The last patterns in this book are relatively uncomplicated and mostly geometrical, as they were worked in the last decades of the lace industry. The first two patterns belong to a group which shows the same features in many variations. The old grid, not with squares but with rectangles, is still used, but the ground is only represented in very small areas or not at all.

Pattern 44:
Narrow geometrical insertion

Wind 26 pairs with 140, three pairs with 35/3

Use one passive pair in the footing in both sides, worked with cloth stitch. Work honeycomb stitch nearly everywhere; only in some gimp nooks near the middle and between them do you use a ground stitch (*x*). Twist the worker pairs twice where they part in the middle of the cloth diamond and before they meet again.

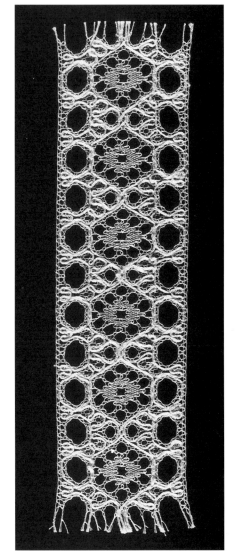

164

165

166

Pattern 45:
Rikke

Wind 59 pairs with 140, seven or eight pairs and one bobbin with 35/3

There is no diagram for this pattern; I made the pricking using a photocopy of a pricking from about 1920 as a model. The first half is worked with the gimp threads as they were indicated in the photocopy but in the second half I have introduced two extra gimp threads, one to make the middle pattern symmetrical, and consequently the other one to make the surrounding of the rose symmetrical. The pricking is more open than usual, but thanks to the many gimps the lace does not seem loose.

As there is no diagram, I will refer to other patterns with the same details. The passive pair in the footing is worked with cloth stitch and twist, and with the catch pin put up to the side of a ground stitch. The way to work the rings and the gimp next to the footing is illustrated in Pattern 44, as is the way to work the gimp loops to the sides of the oval rings; only the ground stitches in the middle are missing. The ring technique is explained in Pattern 1. The little rose in the ground hexagon is explained in Pattern 31 and the way to work the gimp loops (that form the ribbon in the scallop) in Pattern 5. The rings in the scallop are worked in a similar way as in Patterns 19 and 20.

The most intricate part of this pattern is probably the passage of the threads from the headside rings to the ribbon. Be very careful to check that you have the correct number of threads in the ribbon, and also for the rings and for the ground with the rose. This pattern is especially for the lacemaker who really loves to use the gimp.

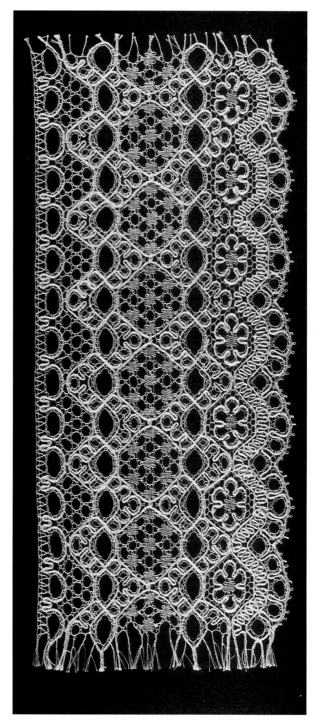

167

168

Pattern 46:

Lace or insertion from a crosscloth

Wind 56 pairs with 140, two pairs: one bobbin with 140 and one with 35/2, three pairs with 35/3

This pattern should really be classified as a Torchon lace, and yet it is something else too. In the honeycomb lozenges the angle for the pricking is changed to give a more circular shape to the small rings. This causes deviations from the straight in the ground which may look incorrect, but this is how it is worked in some ten pieces I have seen, and even in a sample book. In the honeycomb rings round the lozenges some of the pins are moved a little to make these rings more circular too, and the corners of the diamonds are softened in the same way. The result is a

more charming and living lace than you can obtain using a pattern pricked strictly on a square grid.

The odd pairs are used as passive pairs in the footing and the head, with the fine thread at the outside, and worked with cloth stitch. If you want to work an insertion just work a footing on the right-hand side too. Only honeycomb stitch and cloth stitch are used. All cloth diamonds are started in the same direction.

Note: the gimps round the honeycomb rings are worked in two different ways. On three sides the gimp passes round one ring, in between two rings, and round the second ring, but on the fourth side two gimps pass round the rings and change places between them (*x*) (*see* diag. 169). It is worked the same way on both sides, i.e., not symmetrically. It is always worked like this but I have been unable to discover the reason. Do not take away the pins too early in this pattern,

169

132

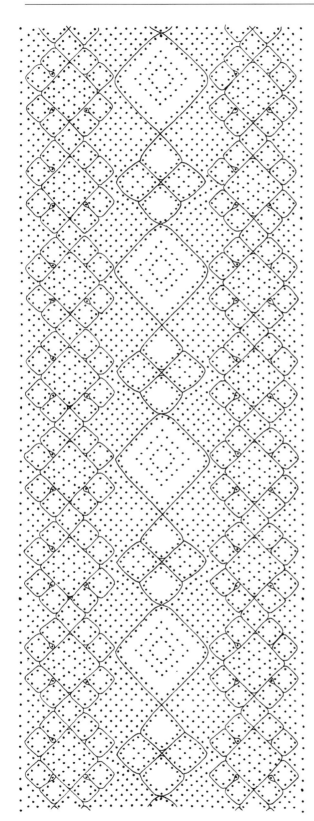

171

especially in the corners where they are supporting a gimp. The lace is rather loose, and the gimps travel straight through the pattern in some places, so you can easily pull the gimps too much and gather the lace behind the pins. It is not easy then to undo your mistake!

170

Pattern 47:
Astrid

Wind 40 pairs with Bockens 50/2

I was given this lace by an old lady called
Astrid, so I gave the pattern her name. It has
been worked in many variations, larger and
smaller, and sometimes with scallops, one big
or four small ones for each large square. It
was very popular for sheets, pillowcases and
other household linen.

First large square: work cloth stitch spiders,
but *note* that two pairs cross in the middle,
supported by a pin. There are two twists on
all legs. All the pins next to the frame and to
the cloth stitch in the middle are worked
with half stitch, pin, half stitch. The rest of
the pins, nearest to the spiders and round the
corners, are worked with cloth stitch and
twist, pin, half stitch. When half of the cloth
stitch centre square is worked, all the pairs to
be used in the half-stitch diamond are twisted
once or, in the case of the two upper pairs,
twice. *Note*: the pin is not covered at the top
and bottom of the diamond. There are
several different worker pairs in the cloth, so
you have to follow how they travel to be able
to pull the right threads and get an even
ground. Between the large squares the two
pairs to the left are twisted twice (*x*), a very
short plait is worked with the two pairs to
the right (*y*), and all other pairs are worked
with cloth stitch and twist.

Second large square: work half-stitch spiders
in the following way: the top and bottom
stitches are cloth stitch and twist, the rest is
worked with half stitch instead of cloth
stitch, again with two pairs crossing in the
middle. There is only one twist on the legs.
All the pins round the spiders are worked in
the same way as in the first part. All the pins
in the cross in the middle are worked with

172

half stitch, pin, half stitch, and, remember,
one twist on the pairs coming from the cloth
stitch. Let the weaver in the tally travel to
and fro about ten times to make a firm,
attractive tally.

173

174

Pattern 48:
Christian IV

Wind 22 pairs with Bouc 120/2, and one pair extra for the corner

Though this pattern is called Christian IV, it is not the type of lace that was worn by the renowned Danish king. But it does bear a great resemblance to the lace made at the end of the seventeenth century. The old lacemakers, who made this pattern and similar in about 1900 said that 'they are by far the oldest ones'. There are many different versions with a cloth-stitch trail as the common feature. I chose this one, because I was told that it was made in large quantities.

There are three passive pairs in the footing, the outer one worked with cloth stitch and twist, the others with cloth stitch. The headside is worked with cloth stitch through four passive pairs, and with one twist on each passive pair and two twists on the worker pair to keep the distance between the passive pairs. It may be worked with an extra twist on the outer passive pair too. In the bottom of the loops there are seven passive pairs in the trail, and the worker pair travels from side to side as usual. When you begin to take pairs out of the trail on one side and take new pairs in on the other, you will get a new worker pair after every pin.

To take a pair out: cloth stitch through all passive pairs, put up the pin inside two pairs (the worker pair and the outer passive pair), ignore the former worker pair, and use the passive pair as the new worker. To take a pair in: cloth stitch through all passive pairs, put up the pin as usual between the worker pair and the outer passive pair, take the new pair as the new worker pair, and cloth stitch through the former worker pair and all passive pairs. At the top of the loops there are four passive pairs, and for a little while

175

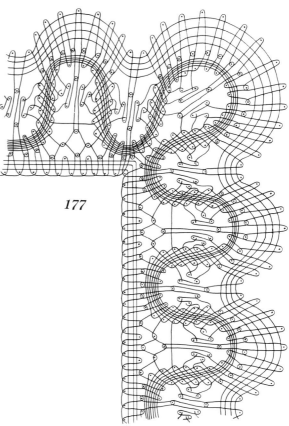

177

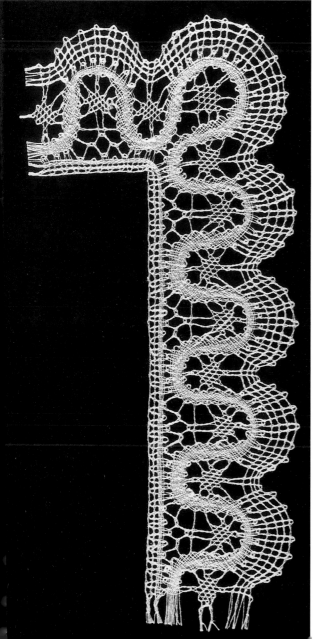

one worker pair travels as usual. In the corner you must introduce an extra pair if you want the trail to have four passives as in the other scallops. Hang it with the threads on each side of a thread in the trail, where the trail is dense, and take away two threads in a dense part after the corner. The foot pin in the corner is used twice, as in Pattern 2. Apart from the half-stitch diamond all the pins inside the loops are worked with cloth stitch and twist, pin, cloth stitch and two twists.

Give the pairs that travel a long way between diamond and trail one or two extra twists, and remember to give an extra twist to the worker pair in the diamonds at every pin. This makes the half stitch look even more beautiful. The diamond may be worked with cloth stitch, and, if you want a denser trail, add one or two passives.

137

176

— 10 —
Dictionary of terms:
Danish-English; English-Danish

Please note that the Danish letter 'æ' is the same as 'ä' or 'ae'; the Danish letter 'ø' is the same as 'ö' or 'oe' and the Danish letter 'å' is the same as 'aa'.

Danish-English

bund, grund	ground
edderkop	spider
galslag	tally
gangpar	worker
halvslag	half stitch
helslag	cloth stitch and twist
hul	hole
indlægstråd	gimp
kniple	to make (bobbin) lace
kniplebrædt	lace pillow
kniplepind	bobbin
knipling	(bobbin) lace
krydse	cross
lukke for nålen	cover the pin
lærredsslag	cloth stitch
nål	pin
par	pair
passiv	passive
picot	picot
prikkebrev	pricking
rapport	repeat
rosenbund	honeycomb
sno, snoning	twist
stils	divider
tråd	thread
tunge	scallop
tyllsbund	point ground

English-Danish

bobbin	kniplepind
cloth stitch	lærredsslag
cloth stitch and twist	helslag
cover the pin	lukke for nålen
cross	krydse
divider	stils
gimp	indlægstråd
ground	bund, grund
half stitch	halvslag
hole	hul
honeycomb	rosenbund
(bobbin) lace	knipling
lace pillow	kniplebrædt
to make (bobbin) lace	kniple
pair	par
passive	passiv
picot	picot
pin	nål
point ground	tyllsbund
pricking	prikkebrev
repeat	rapport
scallop	tunge
spider	edderkop
tally	galslag
thread	tråd
twist	sno, snoning
worker	gangpar

Source material

Books

Aagaard, Knud: *Beskrivelse over Tørning Lehn*, Gyldendal (1815)

Blicher, S.S.: *Vestlig Profil af den Cimbriske Halvøe fra Hamborg til Skagen*, C.Steens Forlag (1839)

Busch, Ebba: *Mønstertegning til Kniplinger*, Nationalmuseet (1980)

Feilberg, H.F.: *Dansk Bondeliv 1*, G.E.C.Gad (1889/1922)

Hannover, Emil: *Tønderske Kniplinger*, Exhibition Catalogue, Copenhagen (1908); illustrated book Høst & Søn (1911/1989)

Kjems, Anna: *Kniplinger og Knæpkager*, Dansk Centralbibliotek for Sydslesvig (1983)

Kyster, Emma: *Tønderske Kniplinger*, Museet på Koldinghus (1931/1989)

Ploug, Mariann: *Knipling*, Den Gamle By, Aarhus (1984)

Rom N.C.: *Den Danske Husflid* Gad (1871)

Schoubye, Sigurd: *Kniplingsindustrien på Tønderegnen*, Tønder Museum (1953/1968)

Wulff, Jens: *Kniplingskræmmer Jens Wulff's Dagbog* (The diary of the lace merchant Jens Wulff), Sønderjyske Aarbøger (1954–55) (extracts from 1813–14 & 1836–58; *Kniplingskræmmer Jens Wulff's Dagbog 1831–36*, Historisk Samfund for Sønderjylland (1988)

Articles

Busch, Ebba: 'En "storkcrede" fra Vesteregnen', Nationalmuseets Arbejdsmark (1961); 'Fra en Kniplerskes Ugebog', Sønderjyske Årbøger (1966); 'En kvindelig Kniplingsforlægger', Folkeminder (1971)

Davidsen, H.C.: 'Kniplingsindustrien paa Vesteregnen', Sprogforeningens Almanak (1909)

Eskildsen, Claus: 'Gamle Lisette fortæller om Knipling i 80 Aar', Sønderjysk Maanedsskrift (1927)

Schoubye, Sigurd: 'Johan & Geske Steinbeck', Nordslevigske Museer XI (1984)

Tornehave, Bodil: 'Regnskabsmetoden i Berthe Marie Alexandersens Ugebog', Sønderjyske Årbøger (1966)

West, Fritz Jürgensen: 'Den Tønderske Kniplingsindustris Blomstringstid', Sønderjyske Årbøger (1901); 'Den Tønderske Kniplingsindustri ved Aar 1800' Sønderjyske Årbøger (1909); 'Den Tønderske Kniplingsindustri i 1840erne', Sønderjyske Årbøger (1928)

Winkel, Esther: 'Om Kniplemønstre', Sønderjysk Månedsskrift (1980)

Zenius, Marianne: 'Knipleskolen fra Nørre Sejerslev', Nationalmuseets Arbejdsmark (1974)

Bibliography

Busch, Ebba: *Mønstertrgning til Kniplinger* (English summary), Nationalmuseet (1980)

Hannover, Emil: *Tønderske Kniplinger* (English summary), Høst & Søn (1911/1989)

Nissen, K.T.: *Knipling III*, Borgens Forlag (1986)

Paludan, Charlotte & Schoubye, Sigurd: *Tønderske Kniplinger* (German summary), Catalogue from an exhibition in Tønder (1989)

Rud, Charlotte: *Knipling efter Tegning 2* (English translation), Notabene (1989)

Tønder, Meta: *Tønder Kniplinger* (English translation), Gjellerups Forlag (1954/1989)

Book suppliers

ENGLAND

The following are stockists of the complete Batsford/Dryad Press range:

Avon

Bridge Bookshop
7 Bridge Street
Bath BA2 4AS

Waterstone & Co.
4–5 Milsom Street
Bath BA1 1DA

Bedfordshire

Arthur Sells
Lane Cove
49 Pedley Lane
Clifton
Shefford SG17 5QT

Berkshire

Loricraft
4 Big Lane
Lambourn

West End Lace Supplies
Ravensworth Court Road
Mortimer West End
Reading RG7 3UD

Buckinghamshire

J. S. Sear Lacecraft Supplies
8 Hillview
Sherington MK16 9NY

Cambridgeshire

Dillons the Bookstore
Sidney Street
Cambridge

Cheshire

Lynn Turner
Church Meadow Crafts
15 Carisbrooke Drive
Winsford CW7 1LN

Cornwall

Creative Books
22A River Street
Truro TR1 2SJ

Devon

Creative Crafts & Needlework
18 High Street
Totnes TQ9 5NP

Honiton Lace Shop
44 High Street
Honiton EX14 8PJ

Dorset

F. Herring & Sons
27 High West Street
Dorchester DT1 1UP

Tim Parker (mail order)
124 Corhampton Road
Boscombe East
Bournemouth BH6 5NL

Christopher Williams
19 Morrison Avenue
Parkstone
Poole BH17 4AD

Durham

Lacemaid
6, 10 & 15 Stoneybeck
Bishop Middleham DL17 9BL

Gloucestershire

Southgate Handicrafts
63 Southgate Street
Gloucester GL1 1TX

Waterstone & Co.
89–90 The Promenade
Cheltenham GL50 1NB

Hampshire

Creative Crafts
11 The Square
Winchester SO23 9ES

Doreen Gill
14 Barnfield Road
Petersfield GU31 4DR

Larkfield Crafts
4 Island Cottages
Mapledurwell
Basingstoke RG23 2LU

Needlestyle
24–26 West Street
Alresford

Ruskins
27 Bell Street
Romsey

Isle of Wight

Busy Bobbins
Unit 7
Scarrots Lane
Newport PO30 1JD

Kent

The Handicraft Shop
47 Northgate
Canterbury

Hatchards
The Great Hall
Mount Pleasant Road
Tunbridge Wells

London

W. & G. Foyle Ltd
113–119 Charing Cross Road
WC2H 0EB

Hatchards
187 Piccadilly W1

Middlesex

Redburn Crafts
Squires Garden Centre
Halliford Road
Upper Halliford
Shepperton TW17 8RU

Norfolk

Alby Lace Museum
Cromer Road
Alby
Norwich NR11 7QE

Jane's Pincushions
Taverham Craft Unit 4
Taverham Nursery Centre
Fir Covert Road
Taverham
Norwich NR8 6HT

Waterstone & Co.
30 London Street
Norwich NR2 1LD

Northamptonshire

D. J. Hornsby
149 High Street
Burton Latimer
Kettering NN15 5RL

Somerset

Bridge Bookshop
62 Bridge Street
Taunton TA1 1UD

Staffordshire

J. & J. Ford (*mail order & lace days only*)
October Hill
65 Upper Way
Upper Longdon
Rugeley WS16 1QB

Sussex

Waterstone & Co. Ltd
120 Terminus Road
Eastbourne

Warwickshire

Christine & David Springett
21 Hillmorton Road
Rugby CV22 6DF

Wiltshire

Everyman Bookshop
5 Bridge Street
Salisbury

North Yorkshire

Craft Basics
9 Gillygate
York

Shireburn Lace
Finkle Court
Finkle Hill
Sherburn in Elmet LS25 6EB

The Craft House
23 Bar Street
Scarborough YO13 9QE

West Midlands

Needlewoman
21 Needles Alley

off New Street
Birmingham B2 5AE

West Yorkshire

Sebalace
Waterloo Mill
Howden Road
Silsden BD20 0HA

George White Lacemaking
    Supplies
40 Heath Drive
Boston Spa LS23 6PB

Jo Firth
58 Kent Crescent
Lowtown, Pudsey
Leeds LS28 9EB

SCOTLAND

Embroidery Shop
51 Willian Street
Edinburgh
Lothian EH3 7LW

Waterstone & Co.
236 Union Street
Aberdeen AB1 1TN

WALES

Bryncraft Bobbins (*mail order*)
B. J. Phillips
Pantglas
Cellan
Lampeter
Dyfed SA48 BJD

Sources of information

UNITED KINGDOM

The British College of Lace
21 Hillmorton Road
Rugby
War CV22 5DF

The English Lace School
Oak House
Church Stile
Woodbury
Nr Exeter
Devon EX5 1HP

The Lace Guild
The Hollies
53 Audnam
Stourbridge
West Midlands DY8 4AE

The Lacemakers' Circle
49 Wardwick
Derby DE1 1HY

The Lace Society
Linwood
Stratford Road
Oversley
Alcester
War BY9 6PG

United Kingdom Director of
    International Old Lacers
S. Hurst
4 Dollis Road
London N3 1RG

Ring of Tatters
Mrs G. Partridge
7 Town Head Avenue
Settle
N. Yorks BD24 9RQ

DENMARK

Tønder Museum
Kongevej 55, DK 6270 Tønder

*Collection of Tønder lace,
    finished works and many
    samples; bobbins and other lace
    equipment.*

Hans og Hansigne Lorenzens
    Gaard
Nørrevej 29, Baadsbøl-Ballum,
    DK 6261 Bredebro

*A private home with a collection
    of lace and lace equipment,
    open only in July 2–6 p.m. In*

the spring and autumn
courses in Tønder lace are
run here.

Museet på Sønderborg Slot
DK 6400 Sønderborg

*Collection of Tønder lace, lace
    imitations on tulle from Als,
    nineteenth-century European
    lace, and a lace teacher's
    samples from the 1950s.*

Museet på Koldinghus
Postbox 91, DK 6000 Kolding

*Collection of lace, bobbins, and
    other lace equipment.*

Købstadsmuseet 'Den Gamle
    By' (The Old Town)
DK 8000 Aarhus C

*Lace in costumes and interiors,
    study collection of Tønder lace.*

Kunstindustrimuseet (The
    Museum of Decorative Art)
Bredgade 68, DK 1260
    København K

*Collection of Tønder lace and
    other European lace. There is a
    comprehensive collection of lace
    books in the library.*

Nationalmuseet, 3. Afdeling,
    Dansk Folkemuseum
Brede, DK 2800 Lyngby

*Collection of Tønder lace as it
    was used in clothing.*

GERMANY

Städtisches Museum Flensburg
Lutherplatz 1, D 2390
    Flensburg

*A small, but representative
    collection of Tønder lace*

USA

International Old Lacers
Gunvor Jorgensen (President)
366 Bradley Avenue
Northvale
NJ 076647
United States

Equipment suppliers

UNITED KINGDOM

General equipment

Alby Lace Museum
Cromer Road
Alby
Norwich
Norfolk NR11 7QE

Busy Bobbins
Unit 7
Scarrots Lane
Newport
IOW PO30 1JD

Chosen Crafts Centre
46 Winchcombe Street
Cheltenham
Glos GL52 2ND

Jo Firth
Lace Marketing & Needlecraft
  Supplies
58 Kent Crescent
Lowtown
Pudsey
W Yorks LS28 9EB

J. & J. Ford (mail order & lace
  days only)
October Hill
Upper Way
Upper Longdon
Rugeley
Staffs WS16 1QB

Framecraft
83 Hampstead Road
Handsworth Wood
Birmingham B2

R. Gravestock
Highwood
Crews Hill
Alfrick
Worcs WR6 5HF

The Handicraft Shop
47 Northgate
Canterbury
Kent CT1 1BE

Frank Herring & Sons
27 High West Street
Dorchester
Dorset DT1 1UP

Honiton Lace Shop
44 High Street
Honiton
Devon EX14 8PJ

D. J. Hornsby
149 High Street
Burton Latimer
Kettering
Northants NN15 5RL
  also at:
25 Manwood Avenue
Canterbury
Kent CT2 7AH

Frances Iles
73 High Street
Rochester
Kent ME1 1LX

Jane's Pincushions
Taverham Craft Unit 4
Taverham Nursery Centre
Fir Covert Road
Taverham
Norwich NR8 6HT

Loricraft
4 Big Lane
Lambourn
Berks

Needlestyle
5 The Woolmead
Farnham
Surrey GU9 7TX

Needlestyle
24–26 West Street
Alresford
Hants

Needlework
Ann Bartleet
Bucklers Farm
Coggeshall
Essex CO6 1SB

Needle and Thread
80 High Street
Horsell
Woking
Surrey GU21 4SZ

The Needlewoman
21 Needles Alley
off New Street
Birmingham B2 5AE

T. Parker (*mail order*)
124 Corhampton Road
Boscombe East
Bournemouth
Dorset BH6 5NZ

Jane Playford
North Lodge
Church Close
West Runton
Norfolk NR27 9QY

Redburn Crafts
Squires Garden Centre
Halliford Road
Upper Halliford
Shepperton
Middx TW17 8RU

Christine Riley
53 Barclay Street
Stonehaven
Kincardineshire
Scotland

Peter & Beverley Scarlett
Strupak
Hill Head
Cold Wells, Ellon
Grampian
Scotland

Ken & Pat Schultz
134 Wisbech Road
Thornley
Peterborough
Cambs

J. S. Sears
Lacecraft Supplies
8 Hillview
Sherington
Bucks MK16 9NY

Sebalace
Waterloo Mills
Howden Road
Silsden
W Yorks BD2 0NA

A. Sells
49 Pedley Lane
Clifton
Shefford
Beds SG17 5QT

Shireburn Lace
Finkle Court
Finkle Hill
Sherburn in Elmet
N Yorks LS25 6EB

SMP
4 Garners Close
Chalfont St Peter
Bucks SL9 0HB

Southern Handicrafts
20 Kensington Gardens
Brighton
Sussex BN1 4AC

Spangles
Carole Morris
Cashburn Lane
Burwell
Cambs CB5 0ED

Stitchery
Finkle Street
Richmond
N Yorks

Stitches
Dovehouse Shopping Parade
Warwick Road
Olton
Solihull
W Midlands

Teazle Embroideries
35 Boothferry Road
Hull
N Humberside

Lynn Turner
Church Meadow Crafts
15 Carisbrooke Drive
Winsford
Cheshire CW7 1LN

The Craft House
23 Bar Street
Scarborough
N Yorks

George Walker
The Corner Shop
Rickinghall, Diss
Norfolk

West End Lace Supplies
Ravensworth Court Road
Mortimer West End
Reading
Berks RG7 3UD

George White Lacemakers'
  Supplies
40 Heath Drive
Boston Spa
W Yorks LS23 6PB

Bobbins

A. R. Archer
The Poplars
Shetland
near Stowmarket
Suffolk IP14 3DE

Bartlett, Caesar and Partners
12 Creslow Court
Stony Stratford
Milton Keynes MK11 1NN
  also at:
The Glen
Shorefield Road
Downton
Lymington
Hants SO41 0LH

T. Brown
Temple Lane Cottage
Littledean
Cinderford
Glos

Bryncraft Bobbins
B. J. Phillips
Pantglas
Cellan
Lampeter
Dyfed SA48 BJD

Chrisken Bobbins
26 Cedar Drive
Kingsclere
Bucks RG15 8TD

Malcolm J. Fielding
2 Northern Terrace
Moss Lane
Silverdale
Lancs LA5 0ST

Richard Gravestock
Highwood
Crews Hill
Alfrick
Worcs WR6 5HF

Larkfield Crafts
Hilary Ricketts
4 Island Cottages
Mapledurwell

Basingstoke
Hants RG25 2LU

Loricraft
4 Big Lane
Lambourn
Berks

T. Parker (*mail order*)
124 Corhampton Road
Boscombe East
Bournemouth
Dorset BH6 5NZ

D. H. Shaw
47 Lamor Crescent
Thrushcroft
Rotherham
S Yorks S66 9QD

Sizelands
1 Highfield Road
Winslow
Bucks MK10 3QU

Christine & David Springett
21 Hillmorton Road
Rugby
War CV22 5DF

Richard Viney
Unit 7
Port Royal Street
Southsea
Hants PO5 3UD

West End Lace Suppliers
Ravensworth Court Road
Mortimer West End
Reading
Berks RG7 3UD

Lace pillows

Newnham Lace Equipment
15 Marlowe Close
Basingstoke
Hants RG24 9DD

Bartlett, Caesar and Partners
12 Creslow Court
Stony Stratford
Milton Keynes MK11 1NN
  also at:

The Glen
Shorefield Road
Downton
Lymington
Hants SO41 0LH

Silk embroidery and lace thread

E. & J. Piper
Silverlea
Flax Lane
Glemsford
Suffolk CO10 7RS

Frames and mounts

Doreen Campbell
Highcliff
Bremilham Road
Malmesbury
Wilts SN16 0DQ

Framecraft Miniatures Ltd
148–150 High Street
Aston
Birmingham B6 4US

Matt coloured transparent adhesive film

Heffers Graphic Shop
26 King Street
Cambridge CB1 1LN

Linen by the metre (yard) and made up articles of church linen

Mary Collins
Church Furnishings
St Andrews Hall
Humber Doucy Lane
Ipswich
Suffolk IP4 3BP

Hayes & Finch
Head Office & Factory
Hanson Road
Aintree
Liverpool L9 9BP

UNITED STATES OF AMERICA

Arbor House
22 Arbor Lane
Roslyn Hights
NY 11577

Baltazor Inc.
3262 Severn Avenue
Metairie
LA 7002

Beggars' Lace
P.O. Box 17263
Denver
Colo 80217

Berga Ullman Inc.
P.O. Box 918
North Adams
MA 01247

Frederick J. Fawcett
129 South Street
Boston
MA 02130

Frivolité
15526 Densmore N.
Seattle
WA 98113

Happy Hands
3007 S. W. Marshall
Pendleton
Oreg 97180

International Old Lacers
P.O. Box 1029
Westminster
Colo 80030

Lace Place de Belgique
800 S. W. 17th Street
Boca Raton
FL 33432

Lacis
2150 Stuart Street
Berkeley
CA 9470

Robin's Bobbins
RTL Box 1736
Mineral Bluff
GA 30559

Robin and Russ
Handweavers
533 North Adams Street
McMinnvills
Oreg 97128

Some Place
2990 Adline Street
Berkeley
CA 94703

Osma G. Todd Studio
319 Mendoza Avenue
Coral Gables
FL 33134

The Unique And Art Lace
  Cleaners
5926 Delman Boulevard
St Louis
MO 63112

Van Scriver Bobbin Lace
130 Cascadilla Park
Ithaca
NY 14850

The World in Stitches
82 South Street
Milford
NH 03055

AUSTRALIA

Australian Lace magazine
P.O. Box 1291
Toowong
Queensland 4066

Dentelles Lace Supplies
c/o Betty Franks
39 Lang Terrace
Northgate 4013
Brisbane
Queensland

The Lacemaker
94 Fordham Avenue
Hartwell
Victoria 3124

Spindle and Loom
Arcade 83
Longueville Road
Lane Cove
NSW 2066

Tulis Crafts
201 Avoca Street
Randwick
NSW 2031

BELGIUM

't Handwerkhuisje
Katelijnestraat 23
8000 Bruges

Kantcentrum
Balstraat 14
8000 Bruges

Manufacture Belge de Dentelle
6 Galerie de la Reine
Galeries Royales St Hubert
1000 Bruxelles

Orchidée
Mariastraat 18
8000 Bruges

Ann Thys
't Apostelientje
Balstraat 11
8000 Bruges

DENMARK

Den Danske Husflidshøjskole
Tyrebakken
DK 5300 Kerteminde

FRANCE

Centre d'Initiations à la
  Dentelle du Puy
2 Rue Duguesclin
43000 Le Puy en Velay

A L'Econome
Anne-Marie Deydier
Ecole de Dentelle aux Fuseaux
10 rue Paul Chenavard
69001 Lyon

Rougier and Plé
13–15 Bd des Filles de Calvaire
75003 Paris

WEST GERMANY

Der Fenster Laden
Berliner Str. 8
D 6483 Bad Soden
Salmünster

P.P. Hempel
Ortolanweg 34
1000 Berlin 47

HOLLAND

Blokker's Boektiek
Bronsteeweg 4/4a
2101 AC Heemstede

Theo Brejaart
Dordtselaan 146–148
P.O. Box 5199
3008 AD Rotterdam

Heikina de Ruÿter
Zuiderstraat 1
9693 ER Nieweschans

Magazijn *De Vlijt*
Lijnmarkt 48
Utrecht

SWITZERLAND

Fadehax
Inh. Irene Solca
4105 Biel-Benken
Basel

NEW ZEALAND

Peter McLeavey
P.O. Box 69. 00 7
Auckland 8